The Unlikely Doctor

From gang life and prison
to becoming a doctor at 56 —
the incredible story of

Dr Timoti Te Moke

with Eugene Bingham

ALLEN&UNWIN
AUCKLAND • SYDNEY • MELBOURNE • LONDON

First published in 2025

Allen & Unwin Aotearoa New Zealand
Level 2, 10 College Hill, Freemans Bay
Auckland 1011, New Zealand
+64 (9) 377 3800
auckland@allenandunwin.com
www.allenandunwin.co.nz

83 Alexander Street
Crows Nest NSW 2065, Australia
+61 (2) 8425 0100

EU Authorised Representative: Easy Access System Europe,
Mustamäe tee 50, 10621 Tallinn, Estonia, gpsr.requests@easproject.com

A catalogue record for this book is available from
the National Library of New Zealand.

ISBN 978 1 991006 88 2

Design by Katrina Duncan
Set in Freight Text
Cover photograph by Stephen Tilley
Wardrobe by Workshop
Printed and bound in Australia by the Opus Group

10 9 8 7 6 5 4

The paper in this book is FSC® certified.
FSC® promotes environmentally responsible,
socially beneficial and economically viable
management of the world's forests.

Contents

Prologue

The Boy on the Crossing

Even when I'm not on shift I have work to do. It's a job that goes beyond the diagnoses and treatments I dispense to my patients as a doctor at Middlemore Hospital in the heart of south Auckland. But it's no less important.

It's about creating lasting change. It's part of what drives me now, after coming so far. And it all came sharply into focus one day, on the face of an eight-year-old boy.

I live close to Middlemore, which isn't far from where I grew up, a couple of suburbs away. These streets are very familiar to me. If you don't know south Auckland, you might have a warped impression of it from the news. Usually, the only time you hear of south Auckland is when something bad has happened, right? Someone has been killed; some place has been robbed; some other shit has gone down.

But that's unfair. South Auckland is a vibrant, colourful place with plenty of good people going about their lives, living their best lives. Sure, for lots of people life is a struggle; perhaps more so than in some other parts of Auckland. And sure, some people have fallen through some pretty big cracks in our society and found themselves in some shitty situations — I certainly know about that. But overall, most people are just trying to get on with their lives; hoping for a break, hoping for hope.

Rather than drive to work I take public transport, bus and train. And by doing that, I'm on a mission. I want to be seen.

This has nothing to do with my ego. I don't get changed before heading home; normally I'm in my standard hospital uniform of scrubs, shoes that are comfortable enough to stand around in for twelve-plus hours, an ID on a lanyard around my neck, and a stethoscope. Sure, I could put on less conspicuous clothes, or just hide away underneath a jacket. But I don't want to. I want people to see a Māori — a brown boy — who is a doctor. I want it to be normalised. I want it to be something people look at and go, *Oh, yep, I could do that.* Or, *Oh, yep, my kids could do that.*

Hell, it doesn't need to just be the kids — I graduated from med school aged 56. Do not allow society to dictate to you at what age your ability to contribute to society ends.

Back to this one day. I'd finished work, and had just got off the bus (in my uniform). I usually go to the gym after work. It's another reason why I catch the bus home — because I have to walk past where the gym is to get home. For some reason I walked right past it that day, to the traffic lights on the corner. I was waiting to cross at the lights by Hunters Plaza — a shopping mall which has been around for decades in Papatoetoe, and has managed to keep a local flavour. As I stood there, I saw there were people around but no one was really taking much notice of me.

Then I saw a young Māori boy on the other side of the road. He was waiting to cross, too, standing with his bike beside him, the traffic zooming along. I guessed he was about eight years old.

As we waited, I could see him looking at me, sizing me up. The crossing signal sounded, and we headed towards each other. As he walked past, pushing his bike, he cast his eyes up at me and said: 'Hey, bro.'

'Hey, bro,' I said back to him. And we carried on our separate ways.

It may not sound like much, but to me it felt like a moment. I could see something in his eyes; it might even have been inspiration. Like he was thinking it could be *him* wearing this uniform one day.

But I also understood that was only part of the story. The nice part of the story. The hopeful part of the story. The inspirational part of the story. The other part of the story was that boy was Māori. This meant that at least one person in his immediate or extended whānau had been charged with a crime, had a connection to a gang, had been in prison. He would have experienced so many more of the negative social effects that society has forced on Māori and the wider population of south Auckland than the realised potential this community has to offer. The harsh reality is that he probably would have done the same thing if I was wearing a gang patch. That single moment affirmed to me that I was doing the right thing.

I wanted that kid, and every other kid, to get to the point where an interaction with a Māori or Pasifika doctor was the norm; where they would think: *That's what we do — we become doctors and nurses and lawyers and teachers and other professionals; even though we might be poor, even though we might not have had the same start at school, even though our people were colonised. We have the potential.*

That's why I wear my scrubs around the place. To send a message. To be the proof.

Because once upon a time, *I* was that kid crossing the road, walking around the same streets. And the messages that were being sent to me were very, very different. I was told I wasn't good enough. I was told I was a piece of shit. As a teenager, I was told to put my hands on my head and that I had a right to remain silent and that anything I did say could be used in evidence against me.

Despite all those messages, despite the myriad opportunities I missed out on, despite the number of times I was pushed down, I made it to where I am today: the brown boy who crossed an enormous divide.

Despite it all. And there was a *lot*.

+ + +

In my childhood, my dream job was to be a soldier. When I was asked what I wanted to be when I grew up, I remember saying, 'To be in the army.' It never happened, though. All my dreams were kicked out of me, and as I grew, I began reflecting my environment. Each day I became more and more of what my environment was moulding me to be.

In my teenage years, dead inside from what had happened to me, I lashed out — angry at a world that, to my way of thinking, had abandoned me. *So fuck the world.* I gravitated to a gang; I landed in jail again and again. At seventeen, the only ambition I had was to die in a hail of bullets. That was my goal — to go out in a gunfight with the cops, ideally hitting some of them before they got me.

In what world does a seventeen-year-old aspire to *that*?

My world, that's where; or at least the world I was in at the time. It seemed my only reasonable option, an aspiration I could actually achieve.

Something, somehow, kept me going, made me think there was another way, and eventually I escaped to Australia. But I discovered you can't run away from the things that haunt you, and I ended up getting drawn back into the world of drugs and gangs. More violence, more betrayal. Danger closed in on me, but I disappeared; returned home to Aotearoa. Finally, slowly, after enduring tests that took me back to the brink, and one that had me dangling over the edge, I found another path. I experienced what people from Narcotics Anonymous would refer to as 'a moment of clarity'.

Now, I need to clarify something here: I have abused multiple substances in my life. I started with solvents (petrol to glue), then graduated to alcohol, then combined alcohol with drugs (weed, pills, acid), then ever-increasing amounts of hard drugs (heroin, cocaine, ice).

And yet, despite all that, despite the haze and blurred outlook those substances gave me, I made another life for myself. Despite it all.

But I am the outlier. I am the exception — for now, at least, though it is my hope that things change.

+ + +

There was a part of my life when I spent more time hanging out on the streets than at home, as well as a time when I lived on the streets to avoid being at home. During those times there was a group of about twenty guys I hung out with regularly. We weren't in a gang; we just saw each other regularly. We were all very similar. We knew what violence was, we knew what poverty was, and we knew not to talk to each other about that stuff. We just existed together, asking nothing but knowing all.

Eventually, we all went our own ways. I drifted away and did my own thing; tight friendships have always been difficult for me. But from time to time I've bumped into some of these guys, and we've caught up about the old days and what everyone was up to.

And there's an awful truth to be found in their answers. Of those twenty guys, I think I'm the only one who's not dead or in prison.

A bunch of them were victims of mental ill-health and drug abuse. A few years ago, around the time there was a spike in meth, a lot of them went psychotic. The outcomes were not good. One guy overdosed, shot himself up and died. Another got on the wrong side of a deal with the wrong people. He was taken to with an axe and found chopped up, or so I was told. Another guy went back to prison after an argument with his girlfriend in a car. They'd started fighting, and he got out and just shot up the car.

I'm not telling you these things to be dramatic or to shock you. When you grow up around violence, those things aren't dramatic or shocking. You understand that's the life, and those are sometimes the outcomes. I'm telling you these things because each of those guys' lives represents a tragic loss to our society. They were guys like me, guys who had the potential for a better life — but who never got the chance.

Some of them were smarter than me. Some were better leaders than me. But they never got out of the life we lived on the streets. They never got the opportunity. I can't help but become extremely cynical when I hear myself say that word. Opportunities come thick and fast for me now. Now that I have overcome everything. But before this, opportunities were extremely rare.

Don't get me wrong, the opportunities were rare for a reason at one point in my life. And that is because I was broken. However, I was only broken because I was denied the opportunities that are the right of every child. These opportunities create a nourishing, supportive, loving environment for a child to grow up in. This then provides the ultimate opportunity that every child needs: the understanding and the belief that they have the ability and the right to be more.

Some people I meet will say, 'Oh, look, you turned your life around — so can others.' It pisses me off. Because I am the *exception*; I'm the one in a billion — ten billion, a fucken trillion — who's been through what I've been through and has got to where I am.

So don't try to use me as some sort of example. It's like doing a study and taking the outlier, and then saying, 'See, this is the result of the study.' Fuck off — I'm at the extremity. Almost all those other guys are the evidence of what happens to most kids who come from where I did; who go through what I did; who end up being targeted by the police like I was.

The thing is, they *can* all make it like I did, so-called 'turn their lives around'. They *can* be like me — but it's not down to them. It's down to *all* of us.

I can show you how we need to do it because I've walked that path. I know where all the pitfalls are. I know where all the detrimental stuff is. I know where all the systemic failures are, the discrimination and the harassment. I know what needs to change.

And it *can* change. I know it can. If we just stop investing hundreds of millions of dollars in keeping things the way they are, pushing people down, and instead spend just a fraction of that investing in people like me, I promise you that the whole country will benefit.

So, yes, I'm a doctor. And I worked hard to get here. But I'm not finished. I'm on that mission: a mission to change minds;

a mission to change things for the better. And part of that is telling my story. It's a story of pain and loss. But it's also a story of survival and hope.

It's a story without an ending — yet. It's a story that I hope influences the lives of others. Like that kid at the crossing. I hope that one day he might be the one standing tall and proud, showing others what's possible.

I just hope he doesn't have to go through what I did to get there, because I don't know if he'd make it.

Chapter 1

Aroha

Before the badness, there was my koro and my nana. There was aroha.

My mum was a product of the urbanisation of Māori. But her life started very differently. She was a young Māori woman, born fourth in a line of seven kids, in a very small Bay of Plenty coastal town, to parents who were steeped in Māori culture and identity. My grandparents had five girls before they had a boy, so those girls, my mum included, got raised as boys. They had to do hard labour and hunt pigs in the bush.

My koro only had one working arm because his sister had dropped him as a baby and it never came right; it just sort of hung by his side. Never seemed to slow him down, though. He would hunt pigs with one or two daughters, two or three dogs, and a knife. There's a picture of Koro, my mum and one of my aunties proudly squatting by a pig they'd hunted — it's huge! I swear it looks more like a horse. It's awesome!

However, what their upbringing meant is that Koro's girls had no sympathy for their own kids. You know when you're little and you hurt yourself and go crying to your mum to make things better? Yeah, that never happened for me and my cousins with our mums.

When she was old enough to leave home my mum followed her elder siblings to Auckland, drawn there by the bright lights and the wondrous tales of the work and the nightlife in the city. She enjoyed all the distractions the big city had to offer a young Māori woman. It's easy to lose your identity in a city, though, and my mum did lose her way. She began gravitating more from work life to nightlife, and then got pregnant. But she wasn't ready to give up this new life that she was enjoying; she wasn't ready to be a mum.

Like many other young women who find themselves pregnant in a big city, she went home to her parents; to Matatā, that small coastal township. More of a village, really. Mum gave birth to me at Whakatāne Hospital. But since she wasn't ready to give up her new-found life for me, she gave me to my grandparents. This is very common in Māori culture; it's called whāngai, an inter-family adoption. So that's how I ended up with Koro and Nana in Matatā. I was born with Koro's name, Te Moke — Timothy Aperehama Te Moke — and my grandparents raised me as their own after Mum returned to Auckland.

Matatā has a stunning beach, a long strip of white sand on the edge of the Pacific Ocean. My aunties told me stories of fish called frostfish that would just throw themselves on to the beach each morning. My mum and aunties would walk along the beach in the morning and scoop up breakfast by the armful. But the beach also had its dangers. You only needed to walk out about 30 metres, and then the sea floor just dropped away. There's been a few people who've died after falling over the edge.

Most days you can see out to the islands of Moutohorā Whale Island and Whakaari White Island, seemingly so close that you feel like you could just reach out to touch them. My koro used to go to Moutohorā all the time, and although I've never been to get them I've heard the place is rich with mutton birds, tītī, a Māori delicacy.

It takes a while to prepare them because they're very salty and very oily. It's weird: my people have been gorging on these salty, oily delicacies for centuries, but it's only since the introduction of capitalistic food production that people of Aotearoa New Zealand, and my people in particular, have experienced hypertension, type 2 diabetes and renal failure. Just saying.

\+ + +

On my koro's side, our marae is Rangitihi and our iwi is Ngāti Rangitihi (those from Rangitihi). Rangitihi, our eponymous ancestor, lived around 300–400 years ago. He became known as 'the man' after a fierce battle. During this battle there was a lull, and each side withdrew and tended to their wounded. It wasn't going very well for Rangitihi and his men. He looked around and saw many of his men were wounded and depleted.

He himself had sustained a serious blow to the head which had caused his skull to be opened up. He remained unfazed, however, grabbing an aka vine and tying it around his head to close the wound. He then ran back into the battle and began fighting ferociously. His men saw this, and it filled them with hope and aspiration. They all charged off after him, and they won the battle. After that battle, Rangitihi was 'the man'.

He fathered eight children to four women, and the children went on to become 'Ngā pūmanawa e waru o Te Arawa', 'The eight beating hearts of Te Arawa'. My line comes from Rangiaohia, who was the child of Rangitihi's second wife. Rangiaohia is the name of our whare tūpuna or ancestral house. Rangiaohia had a son named Mahi, and our hapū, or sub-tribe, is Ngāti Mahi or 'those from Mahi'.

A carving of Mahi sits in our whare tūpuna. He is the pou, the main support post that holds up the roof. The door of the whare tūpuna opens up to Te Awa o Te Atua or 'the river of god'. Our waka, *Te Arawa*, was the first to land in Aotearoa. It landed at Maketū and then made its way up Te Awa o Te Atua. The river has been closed off, so now it's a lagoon, and on the other side of Te Awa o Te Atua is the ocean, Moana nui a Kiwa.

My marae is very special to me. Next to our whare tūpuna we have an urupā or cemetery, where whānau are buried. If you go to the fenceline of the urupā, just over the other side, in unmarked graves, there are many, many, many tūpāpaku or bodies, going back hundreds of years; and at one point in time, every single one of them had my blood in them. I can go and stand there and know that I stood there 400 years ago, and I am standing there again today. It gives me the understanding that I am a link in a very, very long chain. This is what Māori term tūrangawaewae, a place where one can stand.

Through my koro, my tūrangawaewae is in Matatā; and through my nana, my tūrangawaewae is in Te Puke.

+ + +

My nana's line is Tapuika. Tapuika and his father, Tia, were on the waka that left Hawaiki and migrated to Aotearoa. Therefore the Tapuika line is older than the Rangitihi line.

When those on board *Te Arawa* reached Aotearoa, they started naming landmarks — it's a customary practice called taumau, claiming land by discovery. In what is now known as the Bay of Plenty, Tia stood to taumau the lands for his son, Tapuika. So that's the whakapapa of our iwi.

A little side note here: we say we are Te Arawa to denote our waka, but when we left Hawaiki we were actually Ngā Ohomairangi, those from Ohomairangi.

One of the men of Ohomairangi was called Tamatekapua (the great, great grandfather of Rangitihi), and he was well known for pulling dick moves. For example, when we and the rest of the fleet of waka were about to set off for Aotearoa, we needed a tohunga skilled in navigation. Tamatekapua convinced a Tainui tohunga named Ngātoroirangi to come on to our waka to bless it before we set sail. It was appropriate for Ngātoroirangi to do this as both Te Arawa and Tainui were Ngā Ohomairangi. Tamatekapua then kidnapped him when he got on. Then, to make things worse, during the journey he got caught sleeping with Ngātoroirangi's wife.

Obviously Ngātoroirangi was a bit pissed off at that, and so he called up a huge whirlpool to kill everyone. So now everyone on the waka was looking at Tamatekapua and saying things that in that time period would be the equivalent to 'Fuck you, Tama!'

Tamatekapua started pleading with Ngātoroirangi and saying that he was really sorry, but Ngātoroirangi wasn't having a bar of it, and everyone was gonna die. 'Fuck you, Tama!'

Ngā's wife then started pleading with him to spare everyone. Ngātoroirangi was moved by his wife's pleas and called up a big hammerhead shark. They threw ropes around the shark and it pulled them out of the whirlpool to safety.

The name of the shark was Te Arawa, and from that day we named our waka after the shark. So, when we refer to ourselves as Te Arawa we are speaking of our waka, but its name came from the shark that saved us.

I also have ties to the Far North, Te Rerenga Wairua. This is where the spirits of the deceased depart for Hawaiki. Back in the day, marriages would be established by warring factions to bring peace. So it was in the case of Tapuika and Ngāti Kurī. I am the progeny of that marriage. My hapū on my nana's side is Ngāti Kurī, and I carry the name Aperehama from the Far North.

+ + +

Although I was too young to remember, when I lived in Matatā with Koro and Nana I was steeped in te ao Māori. They spoke te reo Māori and English at home, so reo Māori was familiar to my ear from the start. The taha Māori they introduced me to was an important foundation for me, but I would eventually lose touch with it and not come back to it until I was an adult. But like the aroha Nana and Koro surrounded me with, it fortified me for what was to come. The soothing warmth of their voices and the kind embrace of their kaitiakitanga were the start I needed. I feel it gave me strength.

I think my ability to have compassion for people is all down to my grandparents and those early years. Most guys I grew up with in my teens — the ones who are still alive — are still really lost, bitter and angry, but I've made peace with a lot of it, and I'm 100% convinced that it's down to Nana and Koro.

My koro was a hard man, but he was always compassionate. My nana was nothing but love. As far as I'm concerned, they were the greatest people who ever lived, and they always did whatever they could for me. For them, life was whānau, whānau, whānau. And it was for that reason, too, that we ended up moving to Auckland. My mum and her siblings were long gone from Matatā. It was inevitable that Koro and Nana would follow, and so we shifted when I was still a toddler.

I don't remember it, but apparently they just packed up one day, left their house behind, and we drove off. We didn't even have anywhere to live, and Koro didn't have a job to go to. But since whānau was everything, if their kids were in Auckland — that's where we had to be.

My first memories are of us living in a house in Grey Lynn, across from Grey Lynn Park. It's all multimillion-dollar homes around there now but it wasn't back then. We certainly weren't wealthy — we were poor as. But I never wanted for anything. There was always food in the cupboards at home, and they made sure I was warm and healthy. I slept in the same bed as Nana. It was awesome.

Nana was always reading stories to me — instilling in me a love of reading I kept up through all the tumult of the years ahead. She always fussed over me. We were coming back from the shops one day when I was little; I was carrying bottles of milk in a bag and I remember her worrying that it was too heavy for me and I might hurt myself. She was really fretting about it, not wanting her moko to suffer in any way. Nana was always like that. She never stopped worrying about me.

When I started school, at Grey Lynn primary, Koro and Nana would walk me to kura and home again every day. She said I was really good at learning, and that one day when she came to pick me up I was up the front, teaching the rest of the kids in the class. All that reading, all that nurturing, had given me the confidence to let my natural smarts flourish.

Which is not to say I was always a good boy — I had a cheeky streak, even to my grandparents. Sometimes on the way home from kura I'd hide from them and then follow along behind as they looked for me. I should have been in trouble, but there was nothing but love for me.

We moved around a few places in Grey Lynn. My Aunty Becca and Aunty Mona lived with us, too. Aunty Becca was still at college, and Aunty Mona was working and had two boys, John and Daniel, so it was cool growing up there with the three of us boys.

+ + +

While I was surrounded by my grandparents' aroha, and I always felt safe, I remember one flash of violence during that time — not against me, but within the whānau. I hadn't started school yet, so I must have been about four. I was sitting on Nana's lap at home. Some of my aunties and my uncle were there, and Koro.

Then one of my other aunties walked in — and her face was a mess, swollen and bruised. At that time her husband used to drink and then flog the shit out of her. He was a real-life Jake the Muss, the character in *Once Were Warriors* who would fly into a rage when he was pissed, which was often. Of course, it wasn't just my aunty's husband — this was happening in homes all over the country during the 1970s, both Māori and Pākehā. It's just no one talked about it.

For Māori, there were some big social factors driving things. One of those was that many Māori had been disconnected from their roots due to urbanisation following the Second World War. The 'relocation' of Māori was an official policy in the 1960s and it was hugely successful — at least in terms of uprooting thousands of people. Immediately after the war, only about 25% of the Māori population lived in towns and cities; but by the 1980s it was nearly 80%. This was a dramatic migration that had serious consequences.

For some people, in the divide between their tūrangawaewae and the concrete, busy landscapes and factories they found themselves in, anger took root, sustained by alcohol, frustration and poverty. That was the story within my whānau, too. My aunty and uncle lived in Auckland, out west, but he came from a very high Tainui line, a strong, proud whakapapa. However, he had drifted away and just wanted to hit the booze — and then anyone in the vicinity.

Anyway, there I was at home in Grey Lynn, a young boy on Nana's lap, with my aunties, including the one who'd been beaten up. Her husband walked into the house to pick her up and take her home, but Koro and my other uncle had different ideas. He wasn't going anywhere yet. They laid into him — beating the hell out of him, blow after blow, and yelling at him. My koro may have only had one good arm, but he knew how to use it, smashing down with powerful punches. The target of the fury was trying to fight back, but he couldn't; Koro and Uncle acted in brutal unity.

The first time you hear a heavy punch landing, clenched fist on skin, it can stir a visceral reaction; the fight or flight mode kicking in, I suppose. But as I observed the scene in front of me, I took cues from my elders. I saw that my aunties and Nana were just sitting there, nodding. Nothing was said, but the sense I remember was that this was what he deserved for what he had done. It was old-school justice.

I didn't move an inch, sitting still on Nana's lap, but I had no need to be afraid or feel any trepidation. I guess I was just reacting to the way Nana and my aunties were dealing with it.

They were all so calm — a wrong had been done and this was putting it right. Eventually it all ended; everything got cleaned up, the furniture straightened up and the blood wiped away, and my aunty and uncle went home. That was it.

I've never really thought about it until now, but it was the first time I'd been exposed to such blatant violence. And, although I hadn't seen what had preceded it, I had put two and two together — my aunty was being beaten up by her husband. 'Domestic violence', a term that somehow seemed to soften the reality. This was very much the era of 'It's just a domestic' — a thought that pervaded the whole country and all walks of life. Most people tended to shrug their shoulders, to walk away and not get involved. There was no thought of ringing the police. What were they going to do?

Here in our whānau, the decision had been made to leave it to Koro and my uncle to sort it out. Not with a quiet word, or even a harsh one. With *fists*. And no one made a big deal about it — it was just life. That's how things were. There was an acceptance, and I guess I understood.

Not that anything could have prepared me for what was coming in my own life, from others outside of this house of love; times when I would be the one lying on the floor beaten, bruised and bloodied.

+ + +

There's lots I don't know about my origin story. Mum wasn't around much for the first six years or so of my life. I don't know how she met my father, or who he even was, beyond a few disparate clues — I know he's Tongan, and I heard that he was often drunk and violent.

That's all I really know, even though I'd ask, especially as I got older and desperately wanted to know who my real dad was — as if he might help me escape, or at least be a shield from the violence. In later years I'd be having the shit beaten out of me and I'd be thinking *Why isn't my dad here to protect me?* I'd feel so lost, powerless and vulnerable. It was like I didn't know who I really was because everyone else had a dad and I didn't.

In the years I didn't see my mum, she'd got together with another guy, a Pākehā, and had another son, my brother Matthew. But I didn't know anything about them — they were all strangers to me.

And then, one day, she came around to my grandparents' house.

She'd decided she wanted me back. I don't know much about why, although I was told it was for financial reasons. She could get more child support from the government, I suppose. But I was just six and didn't really know what was going on. There was just confusion. I was oblivious that there was a big tug-of-war going on — and I was in the middle.

All I did know was that one day Nana came home crying and told me I had to go out to the car where my mum, step-dad and Matthew were waiting. There had been a court case, and Mum had convinced a judge I should be given back to her. She had married the Pākehā man and told the court that he was my real father, and then stuck this Pākehā man down on my birth certificate. My name was changed from Timothy Aperehama Te Moke to Timothy Aperehama Morrison.

As I walked out to the car, Nana was still bawling her eyes out. I remember looking at her, confused, because she was telling me to get in the back. Why was she crying? Why was she making me do this when she was obviously upset about it? Why wasn't she coming with us?

I was sitting in the back with Matthew, Mum was in the front and my stepfather was behind the wheel. We didn't drive far — they had a house in Kingsland, just a suburb away from Grey Lynn. But it may as well have been another planet compared with where I'd been living.

Everything changed. *Everything*. And I didn't — couldn't — understand what had happened. Yanked out of the most loving environment into a house full of strangers, a house I'd soon come to know as a place of terror and fear.

For the first six years of my life I'd had stability and love, and wanted for nothing, even though we didn't have much. I'd been in an environment where I was nurtured, where there was a desire to educate me and to instil in me a sense of confidence, of knowing who I was. Suddenly, I was in an environment where I was nobody except a target for torment and abuse. And that's how it would be for the next eight years.

Chapter 2

Dead Inside

To truly understand what happened next, you need to understand that I was a child who had been raised in a loving, culturally rich environment, and who had one day been told I now had to go and live with people who said they were my mother, brother and stepfather. And because I had had that loving upbringing, as I drove away from my grandparents' house I had trust that these people would look after me the same way my grandparents did. The true innocence of every child: absolute trust in the adults tasked with caring for them.

From an outsider's perspective, things began innocently enough. At my new home, with my new family of strangers, we were all sitting around a packet of hot chips. The smell of steaming, salty goodness that wafts from a pile of chips wrapped in newspaper normally brings comfort. But to me, the situation was baffling. *Who were these people?* I didn't know. *What was I doing here?* I didn't know. *And why was Nana crying when we left in the car from her and Koro's house in Grey Lynn?* I had no idea what was going on. I was just a confused six-year-old boy reaching for hot chips, alongside the mother I didn't know and the new stepfather and new brother whom I'd only just met.

When the feed was all gone and we'd licked the salt from our fingers, we got up from the table and I had my first chance to take in my new environment — this house in Kingsland, an inner-city Auckland suburb that rests on the slopes of a gully. From the outside, my new home looked like a big house. But it was deceptive. There was an upstairs flat and a downstairs flat. We were downstairs, and some other people lived upstairs.

In our half of the house there were only two bedrooms, my mum and stepfather's room, and the room I shared with my brother. Like the rest of the house, our bedroom was cold, draughty and empty. All the rooms echoed, and the whole house felt damp. Outside there was a wash house, with a big Alsatian dog living there. I always felt sorry for her, chained up all the time like that, so one day I took her for a walk. I thought I was doing the right thing, but she bit someone and had to be put down.

My brother and I had a small mattress on the floor and one blanket between us. At night, huddled up against the cold, things were awkward with my brother, who was almost two years younger than me. We just didn't know each other, so there wasn't much to talk about. We were both so little and I didn't feel I could ask him if he knew what was happening. How was he to know? Besides, I was closer to my cousins back at Nana's house. I missed them. But it was made clear to me there was no going back. This was my new home now.

+ + +

Almost from day one, I remember being yelled at. And within days of arriving, I remember getting hit for the first time.

I was in the living room; maybe I was jumping on a couch or something, like kids do. There wasn't much furniture, I remember that. Whatever I was up to . . . *slap!* I got a backhander across my face from my stepfather, and I went flying across the room. I remember bawling my eyes out, in pain — and confusion. This had never happened to me before. What was going on? Why had I just been hit?

There wasn't time to brood on it for long — the next bashing came soon after. And then the next, and the next. It was constant. And it wasn't like it had started gradually and got worse. I'd gone straight from an environment of love and nurturing to *this*. Trust and innocence quickly became mistrust and absolute fear.

My mother and stepfather used to laugh about it, joking about who I was most scared of, about who could give me a better hiding, which would often happen when they were drunk. I remember being in my room at night and shaking uncontrollably because I could hear my stepfather's car pulling up in the driveway and I knew what was coming next. He'd get out of the car, stumble inside — pissed — and drag me out of bed to beat me up. Afterwards, he'd just go have something to eat and fall asleep like nothing had happened.

Over time, it wasn't just slaps and backhanders I'd get; they'd find new and inventive ways to hurt me, and weapons, too. We had a bamboo hedge and they'd grab pieces off it to whack me with. *Fuck* it hurt. And it would cut me up, raising welts on my body. I can still feel them. Sometimes my stepfather smashed my head through things — walls and stuff, even a window. He also loved kicking me, especially in the guts. I'd be hunched over in pain but he didn't care.

From what I know now, I can't believe I didn't end up with serious internal bleeding. The bruises were one thing, but my insides and my organs were taking a hammering, too. I've seen kids who've been beaten up like I was and then days later they collapse — something has been damaged or ruptured. I honestly don't know how that didn't happen to me.

The physical trauma was only one thing — perhaps you could say I was lucky not to cop any worse injuries than those I suffered, though that seems a horrific thing to say. Mentally and emotionally, though, I escaped nothing. I was in a constant state of paralytic fear, a constant state of wondering when I would next be hit or kicked or shoved.

That's no way for a little kid to live.

Any small slip-up, *whack*. Not doing something I was supposed to, *bang*. Apparently looking at one of them the wrong way, *smack*. I suppose you could call it discipline — that's what they probably thought it was. But it was straight-out violence. Angry, malevolent violence, directed at a kid.

Sometimes my brother would get it, too, but mostly it was me. I guess because I wasn't the blood of my Pākehā stepfather, even though I now had his name. Sometimes I'd ask Mum who my father was, and she'd hit me, screaming and pointing his way: 'He's your father now. He is.' But then *he'd* remind me that I wasn't. He'd pick on the fact that my dad was Tongan, beating me up and yelling at me that I was a 'fucking coconut'. The abuse was relentless, and I felt I just couldn't win no matter what. Whichever way I turned, it was the wrong way.

From very early on I came to understand that these people had no ability or desire to look after me, to protect me, to support me, or to love me. They were just going to beat the shit out of me whenever they felt like it. So why had Mum taken me from my grandparents if this was how she felt about me? I didn't get it. And I really, really missed Nana and Koro. They never came over to our house; I guess they didn't feel welcome. Who could blame them? I sure as fuck didn't want to be there.

Inevitably, I started running away. I'd take off back to Grey Lynn, running through the streets to my grandparents'. I just wanted to go back to the place I still thought of as home; to escape this nightmare. Every time I ran away, though, Mum would turn up and I'd be taken back, shoved into the back of the car. Nana would be crying, I'd be crying. But it didn't matter.

Nothing mattered, least of all what *I* wanted, or where *I* wanted to be.

+ + +

The only small reprieve I got was at school. I loved being at school, at least in those early years. For starters, if I was at school then I wasn't at home. I felt safe. I'd turn up with bruises, fat lips, cuts, sore ribs, pain in my guts, but it didn't matter. I was away from home.

At my new primary school I was considered one of the clever kids. I got put in a special class before school. There was me and about four other kids, and we'd get there early and do tests and solve problems. It was fun and I really enjoyed it. But one day my stepfather just announced, 'That's it — you're not going to that class anymore.' Maybe he didn't like the fact I was enjoying it. Maybe he didn't like the fact I was good at it. Maybe he didn't like me to think I was in any way special. Or maybe he was jealous. I don't know. I just know I was stopped from going. It was always like that: any joy I'd have would quickly be snatched away.

After about two years, we moved out south, to Māngere, and I changed to Southern Cross Primary School (in the 1990s it got merged with three other schools to form Southern Cross Campus). I must have been about eight.

I was still doing well at school, despite the distraction of being beaten up all the time, and the hindrance of hunger. I was starving all the time because there was never any food at home. The cupboards would be absolutely bare — though there always seemed to be money for beer and a carton of cigarettes. A few times I was sent out to collect glass soft-drink bottles — this was back in the day when you could claim a refund if you returned empty glass bottles. Except any money I collected wouldn't be spent on food — no, it would be more booze, more tobacco. Meanwhile, my stomach grumbled.

Because of that, I started to steal. There was one shop on a corner near the school where all the kids would meet every morning before school. But I wasn't there to socialise; I was on a mission. There would be so many kids hanging around that it was easy to go into the shop unnoticed and pinch something to eat. I say easy, but that's because I was a bit of a natural at it. I became pretty good at being invisible — it was a survival instinct — meaning I could walk into the shop and sneak out with a packet of biscuits without anyone noticing. That would be my breakfast and lunch. A packet of stolen biscuits. I was learning how to survive, even if it meant nicking stuff.

My life was joyless. School was generally the only time I got out of the house; it was the only time I was allowed to. Our home was my prison. The rule was that I had to come straight home after school — and when I say straight home, I mean straight home. I was given five minutes. School would finish at 3 p.m. and I'd have until five past three to be in the front door. To make it in time, I'd have to sprint as soon as the bell went. Because if I was even a couple of minutes late, it was an excuse for another flogging. Even if I'd run as fast as I could, even if we'd been held up in class and it wasn't my fault. It didn't matter. Five minutes was all I was allowed.

Once I was home, I was sent straight to my room — with a bashing on the way if I 'deserved' it. It was as if they didn't like the sight of me. In fact, they'd virtually tell me as much. 'The only reason we fucking have you is because we're getting money for you.' Or just plain old 'You're fucking useless.' Almost every word said to me was to demoralise me or put me down.

Was it the poverty getting to them? The grind of life? Maybe all their problems got to them and, in the case of my stepfather, who better to take it out on than some kid who wasn't even his blood? They certainly didn't have it easy, I'll give them that. My stepfather had to give up work because he had problems with his legs. I don't know what it was, but he had ulcers all over them. It looked painful. It certainly made him pissed off.

Mum had to go back to work. Initially she was picking strawberries, then she got a job at Villa Maria, the winery out by the airport. Maybe that made my stepfather feel inadequate, too. Whatever. I'm not about to make excuses for him — for what he did to a little kid day after day, week after week, month after month, year after year. It just didn't stop.

+ + +

As I said, there always seemed to be money for booze and cigarettes. That meant parties. Looking back, I can see how it happened — urbanised Māori, living in the cities, all scattered around, they'd want to come together. I get it. There's nothing wrong with that aspect and, in fact, it's healthy. It's just the alcohol and substance abuse that went along with it — it was fucking mental. Someone would get a keg of beer on Thursday or Friday and there would be a giant, rolling party until Sunday. That was the environment.

There were some good aspects to it — whānau coming over to ours, and I always enjoyed getting to see some of my cousins. Sure I had my brother, Matthew, but I didn't have the same bond with him as I did with my cousins — they were around the same age as me and I'd seen a lot of them when I was living at Koro and Nana's. I think that was the main thing. With Nana and Koro I felt part of a whānau at every moment. Whereas with these people there was never the sense of whānau, and although I had a brother he never felt like one. It was always good to catch up with my cousins and have some fun. Us kids used to try to sneak off to get away from the adults, although that wasn't always possible.

But there were also some very sinister aspects to these parties; aspects that would have an impact on me my whole life.

\+ + +

There's no easy way to say this, and I don't talk about it much. But I got raped. The person who did it tried it again, more than once, but I was able to get away the other times. There were others who I was super-wary of, too, and was extremely careful to avoid being around. But, yeah . . .

I don't know what else to say about it. At the time, I said nothing. Who was I going to talk to? Who would believe me? It had been well and truly instilled in me that I was a worthless, good-for-nothing piece of shit. Why would anyone take my word over an adult's? There was *no way* I was going to tell my mother or stepfather — I just knew that would give them another reason to beat me up. So I said nothing.

The rape messed up my perspective on sex for a long time. There's a lot of things that happened to me that have burnt a mark on me. This fucked me up; it fucked me up big time. My head was already a mess, and sexual abuse made it even worse. The repercussions went on and on. It was a burden I carried, and still do. I've always struggled to have relationships, to connect with people. Because of my home life, trust was always going to be difficult for me — when you've been betrayed so blatantly, so brutally, it's difficult to trust anyone, right? My self-worth was obliterated, my confidence at rock bottom.

Inevitably, I withdrew into a world of numbness. I didn't want to be around anymore. I think I was about nine when I had my first thoughts of suicide. They'd come and go for years, drifting through my head, taunting me with a corrupted illusion of escape.

By the time I was a teenager, I felt empty. I found it difficult to have any friendships, to connect with others. I felt like there was something wrong with me, that I was somehow broken. That I was worthless. That I was useless. I had come to believe what had been brainwashed into me every day for years. I'd see other people having fun, enjoying themselves, and it was a completely foreign thing to me. I didn't know what it meant to be happy, to laugh. I didn't know *how* to. Even sitting with other people made me uncomfortable. I just wanted to be by myself. Not because I inherently preferred being alone — for the first six years of my life, I'd loved being around people, especially Nana and Koro and my cousins. But all that had changed. All that aroha and kaitiakitanga. All that concern. All that comfort. It was gone. Now I was just living in utter fear. Utter terror.

I was afraid of my own shadow. I was afraid of who was going to hurt me next. Everything I did, every glance, every step, felt dangerous. Every interaction with another human involved a calculation of whether they would inflict some sort of pain on me. That's what abuse does to a kid. That's where it leaves them. That's where it left me. Dead inside.

I had lost my innocence and trust, and it had been replaced with mistrust, fear and self-degradation. It was the perfect recipe for the perfect storm that would come to be unleashed on the world.

And when the eye of the storm hits, remember: *you made me.*

Chapter 3

Stupid Shit

Once I was trapped inside my personal prison of abuse, it seemed impossible to get out. Escape just wasn't conceivable — where was I going to go? I was powerless. And respite was a rarity. Nothing I did, nowhere I went, led to anywhere good.

As I got older, even school — once my sanctuary — became a place where trouble followed me. I was the poor kid from the poor house; wearing filthy clothes, with a shaved head because of lice, hungry, fearful, frequently sporting a fat lip or some other injury from a beating the night before. The other kids would turn on me. Kids can be brutal at times, eh? I'd get teased. Of course I would. And I'd end up in fights. Of course I would.

As much as I loved learning, my mind was distracted; I was in survival mode. Now, I found it hard to concentrate. I couldn't take anything in — learning my maths times tables just wasn't a priority. The teachers would try, but it was mostly hopeless. They must have wondered what I was up to, because I'd been doing so well and then it just seemed like I'd become lazy, not interested. It wasn't that at all, of course. I was a mess, inside and outside. How could no one see it; how could no one see I was a shell, barely surviving?

Of course, I wasn't saying anything. There was no way I could even begin to tell anyone what was going on. I couldn't figure out how to explain it. I was so confused — why was this happening to me? And, besides, I couldn't trust anyone. I'd learned not to.

Eventually, I just started to think *What's the point?* I started wagging school from about ten years old. I'd run away from class, or not turn up at all. Initially I'd just find somewhere to hang out for the day, and sleep. Somewhere quiet where I could be by myself, to find some peace, even for just a few hours. Somewhere where no one was going to yell at me, or hit me, or tease me.

Eventually I'd have to go home — on time, of course, trying to avoid a beating for the 'crime' of being late. But I was never going to get away with it for long. Inevitably, the school started ringing home, asking where I was. Inevitably that meant I got more beatings. But it was like I was numb to it: I was going to get a beating anyway, so what difference did it make? So I'd skip school again, get bashed up again. On and on. A literal vicious cycle.

At one point, social workers and the police came around to our house for a family meeting to talk about why I kept missing school and how I was getting into little bits of trouble. Maybe this was a chance to speak up and say what was going on . . . yeah, right. The thought didn't even enter my mind. I sat there and said nothing, eyes cast down, a downtrodden kid amid adults who held all the power. I wasn't going to say a word.

Meanwhile, Mum put everything back on me — going off, and talking all this shit about me, as if all the problems came back to me and me alone. I just sat there and took it all. Not one of those authorities in the room — people who had a duty to protect vulnerable kids like me — thought for a moment that maybe there was other stuff going on, that maybe there was a reason I was behaving like I was.

The signs that I was getting abused were there to see. I was withdrawing into myself, not wanting to be around anyone; I was a great big glaring reflection of the fucked-up environment I was being brought up in. Instead, all the focus turned on me — but as the cause, not the symptom. It ended with the cops saying I needed to settle down and stop misbehaving.

All *that* did was underline to me that I was on my own. There were no rescuers coming to help. I think of that moment now and can see that it was a precursor, setting the precedent for every court appearance I'd ever make; I would act that exact same way every time.

After the family meeting, I just drifted. I started to recognise other kids in the neighbourhood who were in the same position as me. Other kids who were being abused. We wouldn't have to say anything to each other; we could just see. It was like a secret club. You'd be sitting somewhere, and you'd both crack up at something that wasn't even funny but in your fucked-up brains it was. And so you'd think, *Oh, right. You're like me.* Where I lived, there were plenty of kids dealing with violence or abuse in one way or another.

Don't get me wrong — there were good things about Māngere, too. It had a cool community vibe, and there was a youth centre at Māngere Central where kids could go and play pool or do activities. Not that I was really into that stuff; I just preferred hanging out with the group of kids I was gravitating towards. And playing pool was not our thing.

+ + +

Some of the kids I hung out with were excellent at stealing, and they taught me how to pinch things even more efficiently, graduating from those packets of biscuits from the corner shop. Sometimes I still stole just to get something to eat. Other times I'd do it because someone told me to. And if there was one thing that was drummed into me that was instinctive, it was to do what I was told. So I didn't even question if it was right, wrong or just plain dumb.

Once, when I was about eleven, I was with a few other boys at a supermarket in Māngere Central. They grabbed handfuls of chocolates, wrapped them up in a jersey and gave it to me, saying: 'Here, walk outside with these.' Even though it must have been obvious that we were up to something suss, of course I did it. And of course I got caught. The supermarket staff grabbed me, and I had to wait for the cops to come. I was dreading it — not the police, but what would happen to me when I got home.

The cops turned up, put me in the back seat and we drove home. It was my first time in a police car. I looked out at the sky; it was a beautiful sunny day. Our original plan had been to go to a school with a pool and have a swim. The supermarket was just a detour. But here I was, in the back of a cop car: my first time in police custody.

I didn't get charged or anything — I was too young. They just gave me a telling off and told Mum and my stepfather what I'd been up to. From a legal point of view, nothing came of it. But as soon as I got inside and the police had driven off, there were consequences alright. I got a flogging and a half that day. But in a way, it didn't matter. What was another one? It was too late for me to be scared straight.

This was the beginning of my interactions with the police, a trickle of blue in my life that would build into a cascade. Looking back, I find it astonishing that in the beginning they were never coming to the house to help me, or to stop the violence against me. They never looked at me as a vulnerable child or a victim of domestic abuse, or as a citizen they were tasked to protect, like might happen these days. They never asked, '*Why* is this kid out here getting caught doing this stupid shit?'

And so often it was exactly that — stupid shit. Random, stupid shit — as petty as grabbing mail from people's letter-boxes and ripping it up. I can't even explain why I did some of the things I did. Maybe it was a cry for help. Maybe it was just because my brain was messed up. Maybe it was because I was slowly but surely not giving a fuck about the consequences.

I'd also lie all the time. I just couldn't help it. Lying had become natural to me, a learned behaviour coming from the grilling I'd get at home. All the time they'd be asking me things, like they were searching for evidence against me. I was constantly being asked where I'd been, who I'd talked to, what I'd done. It was a never-ending interrogation.

Even when everything I'd done had been perfectly innocent, when I was being questioned back at home I'd deny and deflect, deny and deflect.

'Did you do this?' 'No.'

'Where's that?' 'I don't know.'

'What happened to that guy?' 'No idea.'

I learned how to constantly cover my tracks and avoid telling the truth. It was easier that way. My mind would be frantically trying to avoid getting in trouble and getting beaten up. I became adept at thinking two or three steps ahead, at making shit up, telling stories to make scenarios believable and, in my mind at least, less likely to set off my mum or stepfather. Lying became my default everywhere I went.

+ + +

By the time I was fourteen I had this mentality of constant fear, triggered by the constant abuse; it influenced how I behaved and how I viewed the world. Through my eyes, all I could see were threats, trouble and negativity.

I started hanging out with the older brother of a guy I'd gone to school with — not that I was going to school much anymore. This guy was in the same position as me; living the same kind of life, growing up with the same stresses. So we got each other, on some level, as much as it was possible for me to do that since I couldn't properly trust anyone. We started doing things like breaking into cars. Again, it was more stupid shit rather than some cunning criminal enterprise. But it led to other things.

One day we were in Papakura, another south Auckland suburb, and we started eying up a house to break into. We'd done a few burglaries by this stage; all very petty. Stealing food sometimes, or pinching stuff with no real idea what we were going to do with it. We never talked about it, but looking back, I think the main reason we started doing burglaries was because when we climbed in a window or broke a door lock and stepped inside someone else's home, there was a small jolt of something inside us, something I didn't recognise. A sense of power, maybe; reclaiming something that others had stolen away from me? It's hard to explain.

Anyway, there we were in Papakura, outside this house. Not because it looked like a particularly attractive target, and not because there was anything specific we wanted to steal from inside. Just because. Our thinking was nothing more than *Oh, well, no one's home. Let's jump in the window.*

What we didn't know was that while we were eying up that house, one of the neighbours was eying *us* up and getting on the phone. Next thing the cops arrived, and there was no escape. Back at the police station there wasn't much they could do with me because I was only fourteen, but my mate was sixteen so there was a lot more they could do with him. They questioned him, then threw us both in the back of a police car and took us over to his house where they found a bunch of stolen goods. Back at the cells, we got separated and he got bashed up — by the cops.

Unlike other times I'd been caught by the police, this time was more serious. No being dropped home for a bit of in-house 'justice'. I was headed for my first experience of being locked up — in the Ōwairaka Boys' Home.

Ōwairaka was opened in 1958 as a short-term holding facility for boys aged fourteen to seventeen as they entered the justice system. That makes it sound so benign. But the recent Royal Commission of Inquiry into Abuse in Care has heard evidence from dozens of guys about their experiences there. It was not easy listening. When I first arrived, in mid-1981, I was put into a secure part of the home — a lock-up where you got classified. It was also where you'd end up if you had a history of running away or a history of violence. I had nothing like that on my record; I didn't even *have* a record. It should have been intimidating in the lock-up, but as the door slammed shut and I sat there on my own, I felt at peace. I wasn't scared of being inside this cell. I guess I'd had years of training — I was so used to being locked up in my room on my own. So the silence, the isolation — not a problem.

Something else was really troubling me, though: what's going to happen in the morning? I wasn't scared of the door being locked — I feared the door being *un*locked. Who was going to come through it? What damage were they going to do to me? My mindset was that everyone was out to hurt me . . . why should it be any different here? I dreaded the arrival of the morning and who might come through that door.

But in the morning, I got breakfast, and then I was taken upstairs where other boys were, and I must admit it: I fucking loved it. At lunchtime, there was more food than I'd seen in years, including jugs of chocolate milkshakes and strawberry ones, too. In my world, this was beyond five-star-restaurant stuff.

After lunch, we had a sleep for about an hour, and then we went to the gym. They'd get us to square off against each other. Either solo or two-by-two, we'd sit up on a tall box and fight to push each other off. I was skilled at wrestling and jabbing my opponents to unbalance them. We were also made to get in the boxing ring against each other. I took a lot of beatings, but gave a lot of beatings as well. This was the sanctioned violence but there was a lot of unsanctioned violence, too, and I began thriving on both.

In the evenings, we had dinner — another five-star spread — then we'd play table tennis. At the weekends we'd have movies and chocolates; no need to pinch them from a supermarket bundled up in a jersey. It was awesome. Looking back on it now, though, the place was clearly abusive, and was focused on creating an environment that would eventually transition us to prisons. But with the perspective I had at that time, I thought that this was the way things were and I enjoyed it. I had no way of comprehending that Ōwairaka was preparing and indoctrinating me for a life in institutions.

Of course, I still had all that negative shit running around in my head, and I still didn't trust anyone. And now I was surrounded by kids who had the same shit going on and the same bad habits as I did, so every now and again things would pop off and there would be fights. Or stuff would get stolen and we'd all be in the shit. But overall? If this was what being locked up was like, it was immeasurably better than being on the outside. It was the beginning of institutionalisation.

Chapter 4

A Lifeline

There in the Ōwairaka Boys' Home, even with my liberty taken away from me, I'd found a fragment of freedom. For the first time in eight years I wasn't facing the constant threat of being beaten up at home. Yeah, there were the fights with other boys, but I could handle that. There were kids who couldn't, of course, and I look back now and see that it was really tough for them. But for me, coming from an environment where violence was normalised, being here was okay. With jugs of milkshakes, movie nights and chocolates — they'd even chuck us in the van some weekends and take us for a drive around Auckland — incarceration was not the scary thing I'd worried about on that first night.

And then, someone turned up at the home. The staff told me there was someone who wanted to see me.

I'd been in Ōwairaka about a week when I got told I had that visitor. I hadn't had any yet, so I was a bit anxious. Who was it? I walked into the visitor room and there was one of my schoolteachers, Mrs Mary Kayes. What was *she* doing here? I'd had her as my English teacher at Ngā Tapuwae College (also now part of Southern Cross Campus), but I hadn't exactly been a model student. I used to turn up to her class and fall asleep, exhausted from all the stress or from being up all night getting into trouble.

Mary was the kind of teacher who used to go round to kids' homes to find them when they weren't coming to school and to coax them along. She was a small woman, only about 5 foot 6 inches tall, but she was fearless, and didn't mind walking into some home situations that wouldn't exactly have been welcoming. She believed strongly in the power of education, whatever that might look like — for some kids it was going into the trades, for others it was more traditional studies.

I didn't know what she saw in me, but now here she was in front of me in the visitors' room at Ōwairaka. It had been a while since I'd seen her, and she looked at me and burst into tears, heartbroken at my situation. To be honest, I didn't know how to take it.

She asked me what had happened; I can't remember what I told her, but it would have been a lie. There's no way I would have told the truth — that was something I never did. She'd brought me some books and schoolwork. I took them off her, but, confession time, *I didn't do it, Miss*. Anyway, Mary asked me if it was okay for her to talk to my lawyer. I said 'sure', without really knowing what that meant.

For the next couple of weeks, she visited a few more times, bringing more schoolwork and checking in on me. I was coming up to my court date at the Papakura Youth Court — my first time before a judge. I was charged with burglary and theft — over the house in Papakura and the stolen gear they'd found at my friend's house. Mary told me she'd spoken to my lawyer about me going to live with her and her family, and she asked me if that would be alright with me. I said yes, mostly because it sounded better than the alternative of going back home.

So off I went to court, and in August 1981, aged fourteen, I got my first convictions. I was sentenced to Social Welfare supervision and ordered to live where I was directed. Fortunately for me, the judge accepted Mary's offer for me to live with her family. Instead of going back to Māngere, I headed to Mt Albert in the central city.

\+ + +

Mary had been a solo mum for about five years by that time, with six kids. She'd grown up as an only child, brought up by her mum after her dad had died of tuberculosis. Maybe that was why she surrounded herself with so many people. Because as well as her own children, her home was always overflowing with others — kids she could see were going through hard times or just needed a hand, and so she opened her door to them; to us. At any one time there could be about ten people living in her house. It had about four bedrooms, but we were all bunked up, or there would be mattresses on the floor. This was back in the days of the milk trucks delivering milk around neighbourhoods — at Mary's place, each day a crate of milk was the standard delivery. Not a bottle; a crate.

Mary enrolled me at Mt Albert Grammar, and she used to organise study pods to help us all with our learning. Like I said, she could see the value of education, and she was trying to instil that in me, as if she was throwing me a lifeline to save me from the place I'd found myself. The thing was, I could see the point, and I could even follow the work we did in the study groups. But I just couldn't grab that lifeline. I wasn't in the right space. And so I'd sit there and not say much.

They were the best family, and they loved me unconditionally even though I pushed the boundaries, to say the least. I just kept getting into trouble, and I kept lying. All the time — lying, lying, lying. And just doing more stupid shit. Once, a guy and I stole a bottle of his father's vodka and I drank so much I ended up in hospital, overdosed on alcohol and having my stomach pumped. Dumb stuff.

Another time, I went down south with some cousins — Mary was trying to help rebuild my relationship with my whānau. Except it wasn't exactly a wholesome reunion. Instead, I ended up becoming a drug dealer, almost by accident. One of my whānau was harvesting a crop of cannabis, so I helped him pull it up and strip it. He gave me a big bag of it as a koha, as thanks. I'd hardly ever smoked it myself back then, but suddenly I had this duffel bag stuffed full of freshly harvested dope.

When I got back to Auckland, I showed it to one of Mary's daughters — she freaked out and told me, 'Tim, you've got to get it out of here!' But I wasn't about to dump it. I didn't really know what to do. I decided to sell it, but I knew it was too wet to smoke and had to be dried out before it would be any good to anyone else. So I went into the kitchen and turned on the oven. One of Mary's younger kids was in there and his eyes were the size of saucers. I dried the dope out in the oven, then started selling it in small lots, $10 each. It was total amateur hour.

When I look back, I'm actually embarrassed by my time at Mary's. I even stole money from her. Who does that to such a good woman? A kid who has been through eight years of hell and who has forgotten what it is to be loved and to trust anyone, that's who.

Mary was trying to give me a fresh start, a life in which I could have thrived. But I just couldn't adapt, as much as I wanted to. I was too broken, utterly smashed from eight years of physical and psychological abuse. My head was a fucking mess. So much so that when the court-ordered twelve-month period of living with Mary and her family ended, she asked me if I'd like to stay; and I said no. It seems crazy, right? I went right back to the house in Māngere which had been a place of torment. Again, I can't really explain it. I suppose I couldn't handle the love that was being offered to me because I wasn't in the frame of mind to do it. I was still in 'fight or flight' mode. Mostly fight. I felt like I could handle whatever my stepfather would throw at me. I wanted to stand up to him, to find my feet, to find independence, some freedom.

\+ + +

In truth, the only reprieve I got at that time was through getting high.

Years earlier, well before I'd been sent to Ōwairaka, I'd discovered sniffing petrol. It was an easy, cheap way to lose my mind. I didn't need to find money to buy drugs, or to get my hands on alcohol. Getting my fix was as easy as finding a lawnmower. Even when I was living with Mary, I'd steal petrol from somewhere and hide under the house, to get high and escape my brain. Once I remember how when I came back out from under the house I stank of petrol, and someone asked me why. I said I was trying to fix the lawnmower. Lying, lying, lying.

The thing was, I'd found an outlet, a way to just zone out of everything, to forget the mess and the nightmares I'd lived through. It made me feel numb. I had no other way to handle what I was dealing with. I think drugs helped me to survive and endure. At the time, I didn't have the skills I needed to deal with the shit that was floating around my head, let alone understand it. Plenty of times, I didn't want to be around anymore. But instead of acting on those thoughts, I'd sniff petrol. It was crazy. Incredibly intense. But it got me away from everything, albeit temporarily.

And the high happened quickly, too. Within two or three seconds of inhaling, *bang*, you're out of it, disconnected and hallucinating. Within about five minutes you're back, straight again. Sometimes I'd spend hours at it — up, down, up, down. It was so dangerous, I know. But at the time, I didn't care.

When I got back to Māngere I switched to sniffing glue just because that was what everyone else I knew was doing. The high was smoother. But the intent and the outcome were the same: escape. There was a group of us all like that, kids hanging out together, getting high, and having lots of sex. And whenever we saw an opportunity, we'd break into somewhere and steal stuff. It wasn't even for any reason, there was no goal or purpose. If we found some money, of course we'd be happy. But we weren't out to get rich. The goal was nothing more than just doing it.

I guess it goes back to that desire for power, for some sort of agency over our lives. We were all so fucked up, in various ways. But we had each other, we understood each other. Not that we ever talked about it. We just gravitated together and found a closeness in our separate but shared circumstances, where we'd come from, what we'd gone through. We didn't have to talk about it. No one was sharing their feelings — I don't think we even knew what that meant back then. You didn't say anything. It was impossible to explain what we were feeling. But we *got* each other, we understood each other on a level that others didn't.

When we were together, we just gelled; we found the same things funny, we could sense what each other was thinking. That was useful on the streets. We were a tight crew who had each other's backs because, naturally, there was violence and fights all the time. But we kept each other safe. It was almost like a telepathy; you could tell what the others were thinking without having to speak. And this connection began evolving into a pack mentality.

Sometimes, even though we were underage, we'd go into bars, not looking for a drink but for something to steal.

We'd split up to different areas of the bar, but even separated like that we were closely watching each other. And if someone got into trouble, *bang* — we were all there to protect them. Fuck with one of us and you fucked with all of us. And all of this was done without anything being said. No one had to call for backup. It was instinctive.

Slowly, after years of being subjugated, of being pushed down and abused and made to feel like a fucking nobody, I was finding strength and unity. Mary Kayes and her family had tried to offer me that, of course, reaching out with their love. But I wasn't ready for it. I didn't feel worthy or able to accept it. Instead, I was finding it with people who were as fucked up as me. They weren't asking anything of me. I didn't have to change who I was. I didn't even have to think. In fact, with the glue and the petrol, if I ever did start to think about what I'd gone through, the ways in which I'd been hurt, I had a quick, easy way of erasing that. Chasing a high to wipe out the depths of my pain.

But of course, I was just drifting. We all were. Walking around, hanging out. No school, no jobs. Breaking into places, breaking into cars. Damaging stuff. Inevitably, it meant more run-ins with the cops, and more getting dragged into court, stacking up charges for petty shit: 3 June 1983, wilful damage; 15 July 1983, obstructing police; 4 December 1983, entering with intent to burgle; 13 December 1983, burglary × 2. I was sixteen years old and already I had six marks on my record.

In the eyes of the police, I'd graduated from being a little shit to a criminal who needed to be charged and disciplined to the full extent of the law. Not only was there no mercy for me from them, but they now had a duty to get me off the streets. To them, I was another statistic to deal with.

I was on an unstoppable journey, and I knew what the next destination would be.

Those last two arrests, a week apart just before Christmas, were the final straw. On the first one, I got bail and was released. But when I turned up in court a week later, the judge I appeared before decided enough was enough. The other times I'd been to Youth Court and got off pretty lightly — ordered to pay restitution for the wilful damage and fined $50 for the obstructing police charge (though how anyone thought I was going to be able to pay either of those was beyond me). But by the time the burglary charges rolled around, in December 1983, I was before the District Court, at Ōtāhuhu. An adult court. No more Youth Court.

The judge looked at the paperwork before him, looked up at me in the dock, and said: 'That's it, I'm going to remand you in jail.'

At age sixteen, I was being led to a prison van — destination Mt Eden Prison.

Chapter 5

Learning the Code

Here's the scene: I was sixteen years old. I had lived through eight years of abuse and violence at home, scared of my own shadow and slowly dying on the inside. Thanks to one of my teachers and her family I'd had a reminder of what it was to live in a loving environment, and a glimpse of how education could change things for me.

But all the negative thoughts and experiences had overshadowed all the positivity. So I'd spent the last two years off my face on petrol and glue, trying to obliterate the nightmares in my head; tangled up in street fights and dumb shit; getting into more and more trouble with the cops. On the outside, I was hardening the fuck up. But still — I was only sixteen years old. And I was on my way to *Mt Eden Prison*. And I was shit-scared.

If you don't know Mt Eden, let me tell you a bit about it. It literally dates back to Victorian times, with the site first being used as a jailhouse in 1856. The famous grey-stone-block perimeter with its high turrets and thick outer wall was built in 1882. The last guy hung there was in 1957, about 25 years before I rolled up. So it had heaps of history. Sounds kinda interesting, right?

Nah, fuck that. From the back of the van, as we turned the corner towards the prison, I looked through the grille at the front and my stomach dropped. It loomed like a huge castle from a horror movie; one I certainly did not want to be in.

All the other guys in the van were a lot older than me. Although some of them were talking and even joking, their faces were devoid of all emotion. It was my first lesson in how you did not want to take emotion to prison. But it was hard to push down the fear inside. We got closer to the massive blue door out the front, and I just wished there was some way out, some kind of escape hatch. But I was trapped.

After the blue door graunched and ground open, the van jumped forwards and then jolted to a halt. The engine flicked off, giving way to a brief silence; a vacuum filled with nerves and anxiety. Then the back door was flung open, disgorging us into the bowels of this fresh hell.

Back in the day, those under twenty were in the north extension, a segregated area for youths and people under protection. I kept my eyes down as we were led towards it, and if I wasn't shivering from fear, I soon was because of the cold. It was freezing.

I got pushed towards my cell and then the door slammed shut. I'll never forget the sound. *Boom!* It echoed along the corridor that was now beyond me, on the other side of the door, as I sat alone, locked within a cell, within a wing, within an extension, within this old, cold jailhouse. This was what I had been reduced to: a tiny insect entombed within a spider web. Trapped. I slumped down, almost in tears but desperately trying not to cry, willing myself to keep calm, to be like those guys in the van. I was so overwhelmed it took me almost an hour to even begin to take in my new surroundings.

When I eventually started to look around, what I saw was grim and sparse. Surrounded by white concrete brick walls, I was perched on a steel frame bed with a thin mattress and an even thinner blanket. There was a bucket in the corner. Then I realised there was no toilet.

The bucket was my toilet.

+ + +

On my first night in Mt Eden, alone in my cell, the thing I was most frightened about was the unknown; not having a clue about what was going to happen.

Every sound freaked me out. My nerves were already shot when a deafening din began about fifteen minutes before lights out. Guys were yelling, going absolutely ape-shit, banging their doors and clanging anything and everything against the metal in their cells. The noise echoed right around the wing. What the fuck was going on? There was no one to ask, so I was just left to fret and freak out. *Bang, bang, bang! Boom, boom, boom!* Every strike, every shout resonated inside my brain. On and on it went.

Then, at 10 p.m., lights out. And it was like the noise had been switched off, too. An eerie quiet replaced the racket.

Just like that first night in the Ōwairaka Boys' Home when I'd feared what violence would come through the door, I was shell-shocked in my cell — not because I was locked up, but terrified about whatever was on the outside. I put my shoes by the door, figuring that if it started to open, I'd jam them underneath to at least slow the advance of any intruders. And there was no way I was going to lie on my bed. Instead, I huddled in a corner, my eyes fixed on the door until, eventually, I gave in to an uneasy sleep.

When morning came, all that happened was a rudimentary introduction to prison life. And I came to learn that the banging and shouting before lights out was a nightly occurrence. Whichever gang had ascendency in the wing at the time would sound off each night, a display of dominance. It was a routine, part of the pattern, just like our regular morning regimen — lights on at six o'clock, line up in the corridor for muster and a headcount, then take your bucket to the ablution block to empty it of the piss and shit.

After that most unappetising of starts to the day, we were sent downstairs to line up for breakfast — usually eggs and toast — which was piled on our plates. But rather than allow us to eat together, we were sent back to our rooms with our kai. At least the bucket had been emptied and washed out by then.

At 8 a.m. we were led down to the day areas, fenced-in yards for each different group of prisoners — over- and under-twenties. Initially Mt Eden was only for youth on remand. The sentenced youth were sent elsewhere, usually Waikeria Prison. It wasn't until they remodelled the east wing maybe four years later that the youth remand and sentenced were housed in the same wing. And then there were those on protection. They were the last ones brought down, and everyone else would lean against the wire fence spitting at them and hurling abuse. Protection was the lowest form of life, the absolute bottom of the prison pecking order.

On my first day I stayed on the edges of the yard, warily watching everyone without making it obvious — the last thing I wanted was for anyone to notice I was looking at them. I saw everyone as a threat. The whole time I thought, *Fuck, man, I'm just going to get smashed*. But after a day or two I realised something: just about everyone there was like me. The same mannerisms, the same propensity for lying to cover your tracks, the same inner fears carefully hidden behind a shield of staunchness.

Slowly, I progressed from standing on the edge of the yard to going beneath the covered area where there was a TV, some benches, and a bit of socialising. There were even card games going on. I joined in, and quickly saw everyone was putting their lying skills to good use. Everyone was cheating and talking shit. But from that came a sense of understanding each other. It wasn't something to be pissed off about. Again, it's hard to explain.

In this school of card sharks, we all sharpened our abilities to bullshit more effectively, to lie on the spur of the moment, to hear something that was obviously crap and to react immediately. If someone got caught blatantly cheating — sure, sometimes they'd get a smack. But it wasn't like some prison movie of constant violence, the place I'd feared.

Don't get me wrong: there was no place for softness. Every day there would be a game of scrag, sort of like a prison version of league. Guys would run it straight, right at each other. Fuck it was hard, and it taught you how to be hard: how to take a hit, how to be smacked and to get straight back up and carry on as if it was nothing.

By the time I went back to court, a few weeks later, I'd learned how to be a more effective liar, a more effective cheat, more conditioned to violence. And I'd witnessed how the gangs operated inside, saw how they carried themselves, the politics between them, the rules of engagement, the unwritten codes. It was like I'd done a university summer school course.

I also learned that the inevitability I'd sensed — that unstoppable journey I was on — was normal for many impoverished Māori like me. It was like puberty, a part of growing up; almost like you were being groomed for prison by society, with the police tasked to make that happen. A stream of charges was thrown at you until your fate was unavoidable; until there was only one place you'd end up. You were powerless over it.

+ + +

When I got to court for sentencing, I was given probation and periodic detention — basically like community work. So I was back out on the streets. And I mean literally on the streets. I was at home briefly, but there was no way I was sticking around there. By then, though, being sixteen and with prison experience, I wasn't going to put up with any more shit from my stepfather. I had no fear of him anymore.

I hadn't been out long when there was a moment of reckoning. We sat across the table from each other at home and locked eyes. Neither of us flinched. He didn't say anything, I didn't say anything — but my message was very, very clear. I stared straight at him and conveyed, without words: *If you ever touch me again, I'll fucking kill you.*

He got up from the table and walked away, clearly comprehending the shift in our relationship dynamic. From that day on, he never laid another hand on me. In fact, he never even spoke to me again. Although Mum and he stayed together, so I'd see him sometimes over the years, essentially our relationship ended from this day on.

With Mum, there was a shift, too. But a different one. She would try to talk to me. I think she felt guilty for how I'd been treated, for those eight years of torment and violence, for failing to protect me. She tried to be a mum, but by then it was too late; it was too fucking late. I didn't know how to respond; I was too hurt. On the outside I was strong and intimidating; but deep inside me was still that confused six-year-old kid, the one who soon felt so bruised and betrayed. It would take years for Mum and me to build any kind of relationship.

And it wasn't just Mum trying to crack through my tough shell. Sometimes Mary Kayes would track me down too, still trying to reach out — she even visited me in prison. Once I woke up at some place I was sleeping, and Mary was sitting in the room. She'd found out where I was and had come to see if I was okay. As we talked, she looked around the room and she could see how fucked up things were, how fucked up I was, and she got upset. Once again, I didn't know what to say; I didn't know how to deal with her reaction to my circumstances. And I still didn't know how to reach across the divide between us, to take the path Mary and her family were offering me. Their stability and love were like an unachievable dream.

Nana, too, kept in touch. That same love she'd shown me as a four-year-old struggling to carry bags home from the shops, not wanting me to get hurt — it was just as strong. But I had veered such a long way off track: sleeping on the streets, hanging out with a different crowd of people. There were lots of us living in the central city. It wasn't organised or thought-out; I'd just sleep wherever. No fixed abode, as they say.

That meant tangling with the cops, getting picked up every week or so for stupid stuff: fighting in a public place; carrying an offensive weapon. The weapon charge was such bullshit — it was a fork with two bent prongs. I never used it for violence; it was for breaking into cars. But I wasn't about to tell the cops that. I wasn't telling them nothing.

Throughout this time, too, I was supposed to be going to periodic detention and seeing my probation officer. But it was all a bit hit-and-miss. Every time there was another charge I'd be in Mt Eden on remand, then back out on the street, then back inside. And not giving a flying fuck about following the court's orders. Eventually, my probation officer had an idea and recommended I be sent to CT — Corrective Training, kind of like army training for young offenders.

Big mistake. *Big* mistake.

+ + +

I compare CT with the boot camps the current government has reintroduced, and all I can think is: *You're going to send young people to these camps, and they're going to come out disciplined, focused, fit and able to take orders.*

These ego-driven clowns within the government are creating soldiers that charismatic gang leaders will recruit. It will stimulate the evolution of gangs into disciplined, focused, fit armies that can follow orders. We are at a time in our country where we have allowed politicians without any understanding of what they are doing to drive fear into our nation's people, just so they can make themselves out as the country's fearless saviours. They then create these bullshit institutions that exacerbate every social problem that we already have.

How do I know that? Because that was me; I have lived it. Sure, I was no angel when I arrived at CT. But by the time I left, I was fit, focused and disciplined — but not in the way the justice system wanted me to be. What those clowns refuse to see is that along with being fit, focused and disciplined, those young people — just like me then — are still confused, and fucking angry.

After a long trip down to the central North Island, and a

stop-over at Waikeria Prison, I arrived at Rangipō, where the prison camp for corrective training was based, in the winter of 1984. I was seventeen years old.

All I'd heard beforehand was that you would be running everywhere and that it was fucking cold. Both those things were absolutely true. Everywhere you went, you had to run, and it was 'yes, sir', 'no, sir' the whole time, said through teeth chattering in the frozen air.

We were assigned to these huts where we'd sleep — mine was number 21. Our huts had to be spotless. Everything polished, and our bedrolls perfectly square. In the mornings, they woke us up at 5 a.m. for physical training — PT. Sometimes it was snowing, and we'd be out there in sneakers, shorts and a singlet, that's it. We'd be doing sit-ups, knee jumps, star jumps, for about 45 minutes — even in the snow. My hands would turn blue, so back in the hut I'd wrap them around the light bulb, trying to thaw them out. It was the only source of heat.

Work for the day for me was out in the forest — the prison was surrounded by trees. But to get to our work site we had to run behind the truck carrying our equipment and transporting the guards, aka the screws. It was more than an hour of running, all done in tandem: left, right, left, right, left, right . . . Our job was to thin out the trees, getting rid of the weaker ones so the stronger ones had room to grow. The screws would mark the trees that had to go, and then we'd use axes to chop them down. For hour after hour, only stopping for a cup of tea at 10 a.m. and sandwiches at midday.

At the end of the day we had to run back to the prison, do about half an hour more of PT, shower up, then have something to eat because we would be ravenous by then. We were using so much energy we were always hungry. Food was our obsession, so much so that the currency was pudding — if you needed something, or you had a bet, pudding was the payment. Nothing is more valuable than kai when you're always hungry.

As much as our stomachs were constantly grumbling, our hands were constantly throbbing. From day one, our hands and feet had blisters on blisters from the axes and the cheap canvas shoes. But the screws had a solution — after our showers, we were made to dip our hands and feet in tubs of methylated spirits. It burnt like hell, it hurt like hell; but by the next day you'd have a coating and your skin became tougher. Everything was making me tougher.

During my time in Mt Eden I'd observed how prison codes worked, the rights and wrongs. And I'd been developing a code of my own, understanding what I'd put up with and what I wouldn't stand for. One day I was sitting in my hut when I saw two guys running into another guy's hut to bash him up. It was two-on-one, and it didn't seem right — in my book it was a code violation. So I ran towards the fight and started bashing up the two aggressors. Of course, *I* was the one who got in trouble with the screws for that one.

In fact, I was always getting in trouble. I was always fighting and, as was my way, always doing stupid things. Was I acting out? I dunno. I'd developed an instinct to push back, to not be pushed around.

It meant that my time in CT wasn't easy. I'd get woken up in the freezing cold of night for random inspections, and I had no hope of getting released early from my sentence like others were. There was a system where you earned points for good behaviour, and they'd count towards remission. If you were really well behaved you could get almost a month off your three-month sentence. Not me; I served almost my entire time.

When I got back to Auckland, my probation officer said my CT report was one of the worst he'd ever seen. He was appalled. Not me, though. I was proud. It was a badge of honour. He'd recommended I be sent away in the hope it would shake me up a bit. But all it did was make me super-fit, super-focused, super-disciplined. All ready to go — but I had nothing to go to.

You could say the fuse was set: they had created me and honed me for what was about to happen.

Chapter 6

The Accidental Gangster

When I landed back in Auckland after Corrective Training — fit, disciplined and instilled with a code for my view of the world — I was a weapon. And I was looking for trouble. Well, maybe not trouble as such. It's more complex than that. Maybe it's better to say I was looking for something.

Not long after I got back, I somehow ended up on a huge Treaty of Waitangi protest. There was a hīkoi going to Waitangi in 1985 and I went along as part of a group of young men who would drive ahead of the march to put up tents for the night for everyone to sleep in. Next morning we would pull the tents down, load them in a van, and run them to the next place where we'd all be spending the night.

On the day we reached Waitangi, we marched on to the grounds of the marae. There's a photo of that day that appeared on the cover of the first edition of Dr Ranginui Walker's book *Ka Whawhai Tonu Matou*, and you can see me right in the middle. I'm in a line of guys holding a banner on a white sheet with 'Ka whawhai tonu matou, ake, ake, ake' written on it. It's a famous battle cry which dates back to the Battle of Ōrākau in 1864, during the Waikato Wars, and translates as 'We will fight on for ever and ever and ever'.

In the photo, people are carrying flags for the United Tribes of New Zealand, Te Kara, which was adopted by a group of rangatira in 1834 as a sign of kotahitanga or unity. Most people in the photo have their eyes cast down in front of them or are looking ahead. Me, though, I'm looking off to my right, like I'm on guard for trouble — the mid-eighties was the era when Waitangi protests were at their peak and it wasn't uncommon for there to be raru with the police. I'm wearing a sleeveless denim jacket, have a thick head of dark hair and a scanty moustache; I'm young but I look like I have purpose. At the time, though, I didn't really understand what we were protesting about; I just had a sense that there was an unfairness in my life and that this march, this protest, spoke to it.

Back in Auckland, my actions were often somewhat less meaningful. Sometimes I was reacting to what was happening to me, and sometimes I was just doing stuff that, to me at least, was fun. For instance, some of us would hang around on Queen Street, near where the McDonald's was, right in the middle of the city in a grand old building. We'd sit opposite, just observing who was coming and going. I'd wait for the police to come, walking the beat, then I'd say to the others: 'Watch this.' Then I'd run across the road, hit one of the cops on the head and sprint off like hell. I did it a few times and they never, ever caught me. Never. All that running in the forest, in the cold, had made me fit and fast.

To me, it was just mindless fun: taking a risk, putting myself to the test. But also, I'd grown to hate the police. And don't get me wrong: I'm pretty sure the feeling was mutual. They made that obvious. My only encounters with them were negative, right from that first time they came to our house when I was a young kid running away from school and everything was turned on me, like *I* was the problem, rather than anyone thinking that my behaviour might have been a symptom of the abuse I was suffering day after day.

The police didn't exactly have a great reputation with anyone I knew. Growing up, I'd understood that a person became an adult when they could drink alcohol, and that strong adults were in gangs. I also learned to keep away from the cops because they would inevitably put you in jail. Which was exactly what had happened to me; the warning was in fact a prophecy.

Any tiny chance that I'd ever trust the police, or see them as protectors or some kind of place of refuge, started to vanish the first time I ever saw any of them. It was the day a kid was killed on our street in Māngere. I can't remember how old I was, probably less than ten. This boy on our street was about six, and he was being constantly beaten up at home until it went too far and he was killed. I remember everyone standing out on the street, watching; cars all over the road; and people crying.

The thing to me was that everyone knew what was going on — that the kid was being beaten up, like I was, like others were. But no one had said anything. No one ever said anything about the things that were happening to any of us. And after this death happened, nothing changed. Not even the shock of this kid being killed stopped what was happening to me. I think I even got a beating that day. It just all added to me feeling so powerless and that there was no one I could turn to.

So I never saw the police as people who would ever be there for me, people who would stand up for me. And, gradually, into my teenage years, sure enough I was getting picked up by the police more and more. By seventeen, I was a target. I even got convicted of being a minor found in a bar. In the 1970s and 1980s, when the drinking age was twenty, how many New Zealanders went into bars underage? Heaps, right? I bet only a tiny proportion ever got arrested and convicted for it. And I bet most of those were brown boys like me.

That's definitely how it felt: like I couldn't do anything without landing in trouble with the cops. There was never a warning or a chance to explain myself, let alone compassion or any understanding that I might be fucked up. So, yeah, I acted out. Hitting a cop on the back of the head outside a McDonald's? Not smart, not a good thing to do. But I just didn't give a shit.

Don't worry, though, the cops had their way of getting back at us, and not just by legal means, either. I got my first slap around the head from a cop when I was about fourteen. And from then on, being hit by a cop wasn't unusual. Often it would come with racist insults, too. I'd get called a 'black piece of shit', a 'little black fuck' or a 'filthy black fuck'. On and on it went. The only time I got shown a sliver of decency was one time when I'd been bailed and had just got out. This cop showed up and said, 'We've got a warrant for your arrest.' I pleaded with him, saying I'd only just been released, and showed him my bail form, its ink barely dry.

He said: 'I'll tell you what, I'll leave now as long as you promise to be here tomorrow for me to take you back to court.' I went, 'Yeah okay, cool.' He left, came back the next day, and I was there, and I went to court with him. He was the only cop who ever showed a bit of trust in me. And he was Māori.

Just about every other time, it was a battle. One time at Auckland Central police station there was an encounter that has literally left a scar on me. I was sixteen and had been arrested when I was off my face. If you were in overnight, waiting to go to court the next day, you'd be kept in a cell. In the early hours of the morning, maybe two o'clock, some cops came and got me from my cell, beat me up, then handcuffed me. I was left sitting there not knowing what was going on.

Then I heard the door rattle, looked up, and saw a police dog. It snarled at me — and then they let it loose. It started going nuts and ran straight at me. I jumped up on my feet and turned my back, trying to shield myself from what was coming, suddenly extremely aware that I couldn't do much because I was in handcuffs. I tried to keep the dog off me, but I was literally fighting with my hands tied behind my back. It latched on to one of my arms and I swung it around, using the power of its grip on me against it. We landed on the floor. I got up and tried kicking it.

The cops called the dog off. In all, it only lasted 30 seconds. But you try being bitten by a worked-up police dog for 30 seconds. There were blood and bite marks, one of which has left a scar on my arm. Not that I ever complained about it — who would have listened to me, let alone believed me anyway? Besides, it's hard to explain, but I didn't even have any animosity. It was what it was. They were on one side; I was on the other.

Of course, they had the power and they'd utilise it; they were the state. But I knew that whenever I got the chance, I'd get them back. So I wasn't fearful of them, or even particularly aggrieved. It was just *Oh, yeah, okay. Fuck you. What's next?* I was never going to bow down, to live on my knees.

All these interactions informed my attitude to the police and to authority in general. They weren't going to change me. When you change, you leave things in the past, move on. I didn't. I evolved. I brought all those experiences with me as I grew up, adapting and shaping who I was becoming. And of course it all came on top of those eight years of constant violence I'd been subjected to. Layer upon layer of scars, bruises, wounds and resentment.

+ + +

None of this is to excuse how I behaved. Besides, I'm not asking for forgiveness — I'm just telling you straight. This was my reality. This was how I got to where I was. This was how I evolved. This was where I'd landed: from a six-year-old kid who'd been nurtured and cared for and had all the potential in the world, to *this*. Fuck flight; I was ready to fight. And I did. Constantly.

Living on the streets in central Auckland, there was frequent violence. Every Friday night we'd have fights with a group of Pacific Island boys who would come in from Onehunga, Favona and Māngere. It was a bit of fun, I suppose you could say. Then one night they got hold of an associate of mine who lived on the streets as well. We all knew him. They kicked him in the face and he lost an eye.

We had to get revenge. The next Friday, we made petrol bombs and we waited for them. We knew they always caught the last bus back to Favona from the city, so when we saw it we hid in the shadows and got a girl to wave it down. Then I lit my petrol bomb, and I threw it in front of the bus to stop it from going anywhere. With the flames licking the front of the bus, we were yelling at those boys to come out because we were ready to fight. But the doors stayed shut and they wouldn't budge; they stayed on board.

Eventually we heard sirens and we all scarpered. It wasn't long, though, before the cops caught me. They grilled me about who else was involved. Of course I was never going to nark — I had my code. So I took the rap and made sure no one else got caught. I got charged with a serious offence — discharging a restricted weapon — and was sent straight back to Mt Eden to wait to be dealt with in due course by the courts.

By that stage, even though I was only seventeen, I'd been there so often over the past year that it felt like home. More than any other place did, for sure. Inside, I had connections, I knew people, and I was respected.

I was put in a cell with a young white boy, and he was really nervous. 'It's all good, bro, chill out,' I told him. About half an hour later one of the other guys came past the cell and threw in a joint. 'Sweet, bro!' I called out and sparked it up. I remember the look on the white boy's face. He was freaking out. 'It's okay,' I told him again. 'You're safe in here with me.' Because the thing was: for me, this was comfortable. But for others, they didn't belong there, and it could mean their life.

There was one guy who came in, a little guy, and you could see he didn't belong. One of the other guys started taunting him and threatening him with sexual violence. The little guy was freaking out, saying, 'No, no, no.' But the other guy kept up the threats.

The little guy was in a cell with a guy I knew from schooldays, and that night he'd been sent some drugs. So the two of them got off their faces in their cell. But the little guy was still freaking out about the danger of sexual violence. He couldn't handle it, and somehow he managed to cut his wrists right in front of the guy I knew from school. He was bashing the door, screaming for help, but no screws were coming. It took about an hour before they did, despite the horrendous noise of the anguish and pain we could all hear coming from the cell. And by the time help arrived, the little guy had bled out. He was dead.

+ + +

I was biding my time in Mt Eden, waiting for my court case to come up. I wasn't getting bail this time, and that was okay because I knew staying locked up on remand would come off my jail term. I knew I was getting a prison sentence this time because it was a serious charge. I got a job cleaning, which was great because it meant I could move contraband that people needed shifting around the prison — for a price, of course — and I got to sell gear I could get hold of myself.

Mary Kayes and her daughters would visit me, and with their encouragement I'd read. Anything I could get my hands on — those *2000 AD* comics with Judge Dredd (I loved Rogue Trooper, he was cool), S.E. Hinton's *That was Then, This is Now, Rumble Fish* and *The Outsiders*. I'd sit there and read and read to pass the time away. Some guys were envious because they couldn't read at all, so it would sometimes be like the movies where they'd pass me their letters from home for me to read to them.

It could get a bit hairy. 'What does that bit there say?' 'What does that mean?' I'd have to explain, awkwardly, and hope they didn't blame the messenger as they went off: 'Oh, that bitch!'

My grandparents also came to visit me, and I was always happy to see them even though I was on a different path now. They'd be asking me: 'Are you looking after yourself? Are you eating? Is anyone beating you up?' And I'd be going, 'No, no, I'm fine, I'm fine. How are you?'

I could look after myself; I was more concerned about them. The aroha was still as strong as ever, but I just couldn't reach across the divide. I was too far gone, in a completely different environment from the one I started in with them all those years ago.

+ + +

As I'd expected, I got sentenced to prison for throwing the petrol bomb at the bus; a twelve-month lag. I'd expected longer — something like four years — so I was quite happy. I got sent to Waikeria Prison, in Waikato. It was a large place, with work on-site, including at a farm. Some guys also got to go off-site, into the community, to work.

Rather than being locked down in a cell, I was initially put into a kind of house on the prison site with some others. Two guys who got to go out into the community managed to smuggle back some bottles they'd found on the outside that they thought were alcohol. They started guzzling it down, and suddenly they were screaming in agony, then vomiting, and spewing blood. I don't know what they had been drinking but it definitely wasn't booze. They both died. I was still a kid really, but I was having to deal with all this heavy shit, trying to make sense of it, trying to survive. It was crazy.

It was around that time that I accidentally ended up in a gang. Up until that point I'd managed to keep out of any gangs. There were guys I'd grown up with in Māngere who were in a crew, and they'd ask me: 'Tim, do you want to join?'

'Oh, nah, thank you bro, I've got mad love for you guys, but I'm cool.' And they'd go: 'Oh, yeah, okay.' And it was sweet — everyone just accepted that I ran on my own.

But then there came one day after we'd been working at the prison and I was hanging out on the balcony at my prison house. One of the buses that had taken some guys off to another part of the prison farm pulled up, and a gang member who I knew got off the bus. And he looked at me and said, 'Hey, bro.' And he threw me a gang sign.

I didn't think much of it and just said, 'Oh, hey, bro' back — just to be polite, I suppose. But guys from another gang saw what had happened, and as far as they were concerned, that was it. Just because I'd acknowledged the guy when he threw me a gang sign.

That night, I tried talking to them and they were like, 'Fuck you, you fucking arsehole. We saw you out there.' I tried arguing my case, trying to explain it meant nothing. But they weren't having any of it. So, that was it: my affiliations had been decided; I was a gang member now.

All the rules changed for me; I didn't just have my own code anymore. All of a sudden, I was with this group and had to hang with them and follow their rules. It meant a new perspective for me.

There were people you hung out with and people you didn't. Once I saw a guy I knew from the streets and started talking with him, even had my hand on his shoulder. And then one of the seniors from my gang came up to me and told me my mate was with another group. I had no idea. I asked him: 'Are you?'

He said: 'Yeah.'

'Ah, fuck,' I said. Because I knew what was coming. I took my hand off his shoulder straight away, and soon after I got a bashing;

a huge bashing. Because those were the rules. Fraternising and friendly chats were frowned upon, to put it mildly. So I paid the price. The gang politics that I'd been an observer of, I was now a part of.

If one group controlled an area of the prison, that was the way it was. Although guys would always try it on. One day I was in a part of the prison controlled by another group, not ours. But one of our guys came up to me and said 'I'm going', meaning he was going to stir some shit. There were two lines for meals — one everyone understood was for the dominant gang, and one for everyone else. This guy had decided he was going to line up in their queue and expected me to join him.

Now, the thing was, this was not something we'd debate or discuss. I couldn't say, 'Oh, I don't think that's a good idea.' The code was, if he was going, then I was going. We would always have each other's backs. So there we were, just two of us and a bunch of them, but we jumped into their line. They were furious and it was all kicking off when a whole heap of screws swarmed in and separated us.

Describing it now, it may sound petty. But if you think about it, it's not a long way from politics in any other sphere. Parliament, for instance — maybe with a bit less violence. One group has the upper hand, the other group pushes the boundaries, tries to gain ascendancy; and if they've got the numbers, they win. If they don't, they lose. Deals are made, deals are broken. There are flare-ups, and there are no-go areas.

Meanwhile, for individuals within a group, it doesn't necessarily matter what *you* want, you must go along with what your group says. If they believe something, you believe it. If they want something, you want something. The strength is in the numbers. Sometimes those numbers go your way, and sometimes those numbers are very much against you. As I was to find out.

Chapter 7

A New Beginning

There are things I won't say about what it was like to be in a gang. There are thousands of stories about that life. I feel like that story is not my story to tell. However, there *are* things that happened to me, experiences I went through, that give an insight into me and how I've ended up where I have. They'll also help me explain why I think gangs have a place in this country and why the usual policies to tear them down will never work.

I'll give you an example of something that will demonstrate why I think that. It's an incident that happened one of the times I was in Mt Eden on remand; an incident that illustrates my single-minded focus, and the attitude within gangs that you never, ever back down. I was eighteen years old, waiting all night in the dark of my cell, preparing to fight and prepared to die. I'd torn the legs off my bed to use as a club, ripped up the mattress from my bed and wrapped it around my body to soften any blows, had a toothbrush sharpened up as a rudimentary but hopefully effective weapon in my hand, as well as a shoe ready to shove under the door to slow the progress of the likely invaders. I was ready; as ready as I'd ever been. *If I die, some of you fuckers are coming with me,* I thought to myself.

The build-up to this night had started a few days before. I'd been sitting at a bench in a concrete cubicle in the east wing. This was when the remodelling of the prison had happened. Under-twenties, both remand and sentenced, were now in the east wing with the sentenced on the bottom landing and the remand on the top landing. The day yards were separate. I was playing the card game Euchre with some guys when I heard noises behind me — heavy footfalls, *dum, dum, dum, dum.* I turned around and saw five guys from another gang had jumped over a wall — and I didn't have to be a rocket scientist to know they were there for me. Four of the guys were from one gang. And with them was another guy — he had been on the bus I'd thrown the petrol bomb at. They all started taunting me to come and fight. I looked across at the guys I was playing cards with and said, 'I'll catch you later.' As I walked out into the yard, I thought: *Yeah, this is gonna hurt.*

They were indeed there to deal with me. And they did; I got a hell of a beating. By the time the screws arrived to pull them off me, plenty of damage had been done so I was taken to the prison infirmary. After I got fixed up and had been given all the painkillers I could get away with asking for, the prison bosses wanted to send me to the protection block. They figured the other gang would want to finish off what they'd started. And they were right to think that.

'Fuck off, man, I'm not going to protection,' I told them.

'But they'll kill you,' the screws replied.

'I'm not going.' I was willing to die rather than be a fucking coward and go to protection. It wasn't that I wanted to die; it's just that I was never ready to back down or avoid what was coming to me. There was no fear.

Side note: if any politician thinks that telling a gang member to 'take off their patch or else' will have any impact at all, they are deluded. The only response will be 'Or else *what*?' Push someone like that into a corner, and you can't expect them to just lie down and take it.

Anyway, off I went, back to the yard. Later, I was sitting in my cell when the guy I'd thrown the petrol bomb at came in to speak to me. I reckon I need to explain that, too: despite what you might think, prison gangs are not constantly engaged in violence. There can be moments of nuance and calm when there are discussions and arrangement. One moment it can be full-on and hyper-violent with everyone brimming with murderous intent, and then the next day the smoke has cleared away and it's like it never happened. Everyone has to live together, after all.

So there I was with this guy. He'd come to ask me what was happening, why I was there. I told him I was due in court the next day, and I'd probably end up back inside. What this meant was, if I got sentenced back to 'the Mount' I would be coming back here but this time I'd be downstairs where the sentenced people were. 'Here's the thing,' he explained to me. 'We're cool now, but the guys downstairs? They want to kill you.'

Although he didn't say it directly, I knew they would be discussing right now whether to come for me before I went to court, or wait for me to return . . . and come to them. This was why I was spending the night sitting in my cell armed up and ready to fight for my life.

Come morning, I heard the guards' footsteps along the corridor and the jangle of keys as our cell doors were unlocked. *Here we go*, I thought. *Those guys will be charging up the stairs to my cell any minute.* And I waited, and I waited . . . but the attackers never came. I guessed they thought it would be easier to wait for me to come back.

Off I headed to face the judge, expecting to be sent back to Mt Eden. But, for one of the few times in my life, it worked out well for me. Somehow the case needed to be remanded. I got bail, and walked out of the court. So I was saved.

+ + +

Saved is the right word for what happened that time. It was the timely — albeit coincidental — intervention of the judge that stopped me getting fucking killed. But mostly, when I somehow escaped dangerous situations in my life, 'saved' is not the right word. Being saved implies something passive, something that happened to me. Most of the time, though, I got out of situations because of something inside me that drove me to do so.

Often it was just a will to live — I didn't want to die. Don't get me wrong; there were plenty of times when I did have suicidal thoughts, but they never took root. I'd be heading into a spiral, thinking about some of the things that had happened to me, fucked-up thoughts flying through my head; I'd reach for something to get me high, inhale it, and the thoughts would shake loose.

It's hard to explain this thing inside me that drove me to get out of situations, or to find another way. I don't know what it was. But there are a couple of times in my life when it was an obvious presence. Here's an example. I was in Waikeria Prison, in my cell, only eighteen but already well and truly institutionalised. I felt more comfortable in jail than I did outside.

I had a month to go on my lag. My cellmate and I had some weed and we'd sparked it up. I was off my fucking face, absolutely zoned. I looked up towards a thick glass window which was behind steel bars, and I could see the sky. But it looked different. I'd never seen anything so brilliant in all my life. It was stunning and wondrous. That's all I was thinking about. But then, a thought popped into my head; out of the blue, you could say: *Next time I'm back inside, I'm never leaving.* It wasn't a morbid or depressing thought, just a realisation that this was my life: the cops were going to keep hounding me until they got me on something serious, or I ended up killing someone.

And then another thought appeared: *It doesn't have to be that way.* There was no big flash of light, no thunderbolts or any

'Come to Jesus' thing. Just a realisation. A response — from somewhere — to my previous thought.

I can't explain why it happened. But it stuck with me. *Huh, it really doesn't have to be this way.*

In stories like mine, people are always looking for 'the moment'. The exact minute when things changed forever. I'm here to tell you: that's bullshit. It doesn't work that way. Life isn't a fairytale. There is no Hollywood script. Choirs of angels don't suddenly appear. But for sure, when I look back, this was a critical episode, one where something prompted me to reconsider my ways, what was happening with my life. Of course it's not the case that from that moment on, everything changed in an instant and stayed that way. It's not like I stubbed out the joint, went clean and lived happily ever after. It's more like something started smouldering, a slow evolution beginning to unfold. The seeds had been planted, if you like.

At the end of that prison sentence, I went back to Auckland and, from the outside, it looked like nothing much changed. I was still in the gang, I was still getting in drug-induced trouble, still getting arrested. But I was disgruntled with being part of the gang. You know those break-up conversations which go 'It's not you, it's me'? That was how I was feeling. I had nothing against the group. It just wasn't the life I wanted. I thought, *Nah, this isn't me* — even though, when I was in I was 100% in, I was willing to die for them. But I'd always been a loner, and I wanted to go back to that.

So, after about a year of mulling things over, I went to the leaders and said: 'I'm leaving.' That's about the last thing I remember. I got a beating, and it cost me some time in hospital. You'll never hear me complain about that, though. Those were the rules. That was what I had signed up to, a price I always knew I would have to pay. There's no evolution without consequences.

I bear no animosity, and in fact I see some of the bros around from time to time and we'll have a kōrero. No hard feelings.

\+ + +

Reflecting on my time in the gang, I can see how it helped me begin to find my identity, to understand that I wasn't alone in feeling targeted, and to figure out that the way society saw me was nothing personal — it was the way society and our dysfunctional system saw *everyone* who was like me.

What do I mean by that? I realised that all this hatred I felt was directed towards me, all the resources put in to locking me up in prison, to taking away my liberty, to make me less than what I was — it was happening to a whole group of us. And who was 'us'? Let me put it like this: how many well-educated people end up in gangs, end up in prison? How many wealthy people end up in gangs? How many people whose parents own a house end up in gangs? Fuck all, that's how many. And how many of the people who end up in gangs, end up in prisons, are brown? Is that a coincidence?

Being in the gang gave me a moment in time when I came to terms with where I was from and what I was dealing with, and could see that society was tilted against us; that there were those who sought to manipulate the system and the laws of this country to subjugate us and prevent us from succeeding. I saw the biases within education, within employment, within health, within housing, within justice.

Time and again, the mentality of many politicians is to 'crack down' on gangs, to lock up gang members as if just doing that solves the problem. Guess what? It doesn't. Gangs reflect society and its cancers; they are like a mirror of what's going on, the downfalls and the problems. You can't just lock 'em up and look away. That doesn't fix the conditions that help gangs thrive, it doesn't mitigate against the prejudices inherent in our country. If you ban patches and lock people up, all you're doing is throwing a cover over the mirror. It fixes nothing. Oh, and by the way, you think that taking a patch off someone is going to stop them being intimidating? Give me a break. It will push people closer together, strengthen their unity against the oppressor.

Being in the gang gave me a sense of belonging. To a kid who grew up poor, who grew up being abused, who was being arrested all the time and getting smacked around and racially abused by cops, of course it was attractive. Within the gang, I perceived the sense of unity as love and admiration. It wasn't, but is it any wonder I was confused?

+ + +

Having decided that gang life was not for me and that I wanted something else — needed something else — I had a decision to make. What was it I was looking for? I had no idea.

I started doing odd jobs around Auckland, then got put on a government work scheme: a twelve-week course to help me find a job. Out of that I got some interviews and landed an apprenticeship on a building site. I actually helped build the Westfield mall in Newmarket. If you take down some of the panels on the walls, you'll find my name written inside.

Initially things went well. I enjoyed the work, and there was a good bunch of guys. But underneath it all I was still a mess, still fucked up by all the things in my head. I hadn't dealt with any of it. And so I still had that urge to feel numb, to avoid thinking about shit. I'd get together with mates at the weekend and get off my face.

Things deteriorated. A guy turned up on site who I knew — the guy from another gang whose shoulder I'd put my hand on in prison. We were both out of the gangs now and trying to stay on the straight and narrow. But the bad habits started coming back. I wasn't just boozing during the weekends any more — we were getting off our faces every night. I started not turning up for work, and things went downhill rapidly.

More stupid shit; more stupid convictions; more petty attention from the cops with no sign they'd ever give me a break. My record started stacking up again: disorderly behaviour, littering (I accidentally dropped a whisky bottle) and, would you believe it, 'insulting language'. Yes, that's an actual crime, for which I got taken to court and fined $75. Fuck me.

Then the guy I'd started hanging out with got locked up for breaking into a house — it was an early 'home invasion', before anyone knew what that was. It was a bit of a wake-up call for me.

I couldn't see things ending well in the situation I was in, on this downhill slide. There was only one future I could see: sooner or later, I was going to end up back in prison for a long, long time. It was time for another restart.

That internal imperative driving me to get out, to find another life, kicked in again. I made a split-second decision: I had some money, so I quit my job and went to Australia with another guy. I was twenty-one. We jumped off the plane in Sydney and I was carrying a small army bag with some jeans, some shorts, underpants and socks and that was about it. I didn't have much of an idea about what I was going to do. We headed to a backpackers for the night, then the next day hit the streets looking for work.

I got the odd labouring job, but it was tough being without steady work. And I discovered that being in a different country didn't mean I'd be any further away from the mess in my head. So I started acting up again, a little of the same shit in a different country. About three weeks after we landed, I went out with the guy I'd come over with and another Kiwi, and we got off our faces. By the end of the night I was out of it and trying to break into a car. At the time, it made total sense — we had no money left, so how else were we going to get home? The police had other ideas, and I got arrested.

I spent a few days in the cells at the Newtown police station. Like I said, same shit, different country. I got bailed to the place we were staying at, a flat with this cool Greek guy. As my court date approached, I thought, *Fuck this — let's get out of here.* So we took off to Melbourne. I never did go to court in Sydney.

In Melbourne, we stayed with some friends of my mate's in this big party house. I'd discovered that Australia was another scene altogether for drugs. You could easily get your hands on anything, so I started experimenting with all sorts. It was wild, and it became a theme of my time in Australia, especially early on.

The guy I'd come across with decided Australia was not for him, so he moved back home. But I stayed on and started settling in a bit, getting plenty of work and earning some good money — re-stumping old houses, putting up fences around industrial sites, furniture removal. I was pocketing about $150 a day, a decent amount in those days, but I was spending almost all of it on drugs. The more I used, the higher my tolerance got.

I moved back up to Sydney and found some removal work with a guy I knew. He was really into his drugs as well, so we worked hard and partied harder. I didn't really drink, but I was using heavy drugs. Heroin to chill me out and relax me, and lines of cocaine to get me going. It really helped with the furniture moving — which was good because I'd developed a really expensive habit so I *needed* to be working.

The drug culture in Sydney at the time was crazy. Having drugs was like having a cup of tea. You'd go around to someone's house, and they wouldn't put the kettle on — they'd pull out some shit. There were heaps of junkies around, and I'd look at them — never looking down at them, though — and think, *I don't want to end up like that*. Life was good, but I was living on an edge I knew I didn't want to fall over.

You know what happened next, right?

Chapter 8

Heading to Rehab

To my way of thinking, life in Sydney was going well. Steady work doing furniture removals, and partying. I'd left behind the violence and turmoil of my childhood, but, in truth, it hadn't left me; it was still lurking there in my head. Experimenting with all the drugs on offer helped, or so I thought. It was like I'd reached a place where as long as I could keep moving forward, and not look backwards, I'd be okay. But it still didn't feel a safe place to be.

A bit of a hiccup came when the guy who owned the removal company decided to pack up and move to Thailand. His plan was to live on the beach and get shit-faced every day. Without steady work, I was in a precarious position again. Things were okay for a few months — I ended up boarding with some guys who were foreign students studying in Sydney. They were sound engineers and really into music, so we'd go to open-mic concerts, or do a lot of sitting around listening to music while getting wasted. Crucially, they weren't into hard drugs, just weed and alcohol, so in that sense they were a good influence on me. But then they finished their studies and headed home. I had to find somewhere else to live.

The next place I landed was nowhere near as good for me. In fact, it had me hitting rock bottom pretty quickly. Those junkies I used to see around the streets of Sydney? Yeah, I ended up in a junkie house.

I knew them through the guy I used to work for — that's where he got heroin from — and they invited me to come and stay after hearing I had nowhere to go; in their heads, I was their next meal ticket. That's why junkies are always happy to give you the first taste: because you're going to like it and they're the only ones who can get it for you. Inviting me to stay with them was giving me an invitation to be trapped. But I couldn't see that.

Quickly, though, I was caught up in a venomous snare, hooked on heroin. I'll be honest: as far as the sensation went, I fucking loved it. Within 10 to 15 seconds the high started coming on, and within 45 seconds you'd feel like you were in an intense, warm hug. That was such a foreign feeling to me; something I'd missed, a sensation I hadn't experienced since I was a little boy living with Nana and Koro. But that was as wholesome as it got.

Once I was off the high, all I could think about — all any of us in the house could think about — was where the next hit was coming from. Everyone's existence was based on that one desire, overlaid with a thick slathering of paranoia. We were all suspicious of each other, and for good reason. No one could be trusted. I used to joke: there's an alcoholic and a junkie, which one will steal your wallet? They both will, but the junkie will help you look for it. Duplicity and cunning were the overwhelming vibes. If you could get one over someone else in the house, more fool them. Otherwise, you'd be out looking for money elsewhere. The guys would go off and steal things to sell, the women sold their bodies. Each day I got up and headed out to rob stuff, fiendishly trying to scrape together some cash. It became my routine.

But then I had a moment like I'd had in Waikeria Prison, looking out the window to that blue, blue sky. I realised I was so hooked into this poisonous cycle — crime, high, crime, high, crime, high — that it was not going to end well. I knew myself too well, knew that I would just keep going and going until I did something big, and then I'd *really* be in the shit.

That thing inside me that once before had made me think about another direction piped up again. Once more, I thought: *It doesn't have to be like this*. It was like I was looking through that prison window again, a portal to a life beyond.

+ + +

Just like before, I had no idea what that other life was — yet. I just knew things had to change. This time around, I moved a bit more quickly.

I had $100, usually destined for one thing only — my next score. Instead, before I could change my mind, I acted on my new plan. Without saying anything to anybody else, I slipped out the door and headed to the train station. I asked the guy at the ticket stand how far away I could get with $100. 'Adelaide,' he said. I'd never been to Adelaide, but I knew someone from there and had his number. So, before I could change my mind, I said, 'Yep, I'll take a ticket, please. One way.'

Sitting on the train out of Sydney, I could feel the toxic shit of that whole environment dripping off me with each clickety-clack of the wheels on the railway lines. It felt good to be getting as far away as possible from it, leaving behind a situation I knew would have a bad ending. But I was far from safe. For starters, I had no idea what I was going to do. It was lucky I had hours to think about it and come up with a plan.

As soon as I arrived, I rang the guy I knew in Adelaide and told him I was in town. 'Cool — come on over,' he said. It was the middle of the day, but we went to the beach. Sounds pleasant, right, but being out in the South Australian sun was like standing in front of a roaring furnace. It was New Year's Eve, so we went out to a party and got wasted, drinking heaps and maybe even having drugs. I can't quite remember. As far as I was concerned, though, this was one last blow-out, one last party. The next day, I went through with something I'd thought about on the train: time to get clean. I had to give myself a chance. I had to make a break and cut this vicious cycle.

And so I headed to the Salvation Army Bridge programme in Adelaide. A new year, 1990; a new start. Getting clean was my only hope. At the time, though, the Salvation Army programme was only for alcoholics. My problem was drugs. Addiction, for me, wasn't so much about what I was taking, it was *why* I was taking it. Right now, drugs were masking lots of my problems and also landing me in trouble. At times, alcohol could do that; though other times I could drink without spinning out of control — it depended on *why* I'd be using it. But right now, the drugs were the issue.

At the Bridge programme they could see I needed help, so they let me stay for a couple of weeks while they found me a place on a drug rehab programme. I really needed it — I was an addict. I stayed in my room as I went through massive withdrawals — nausea, sweats, throwing up, not being able to sleep . . . I was a total mess for about three days. After that, I was dead tired, like a deflated balloon. There was nothing.

Well, nothing but the demons I'd been using drugs to hide from. With the numbness gone, I was alone with the thoughts I'd been running away from for years. It was terrifying. I could understand why it was so hard for some people to go clean. But my mind was made up.

+ + +

A space became available for me at a residential drug rehabilitation centre called The Woolshed, on a big rural property. It was in the Adelaide Hills, about an hour's drive out of the city along country roads lined with huge red gum trees. The place got its name because of the big old former woolshed where we had our meals and group meetings. It had a large kitchen and dining area and a bunch of couches and TVs. We also did yoga and meditation in there — I'd never done that before and it was fucking hard, but I loved it.

There were about 30 of us residents and we were split up into four cabins where we slept each night. The cabins had Aussie names like Jumbuck. In the fields around them were vegetable gardens where we grew what we could to be as self-sufficient as possible. We needed to do that because we didn't have much money each week to buy food with. We were paid a sickness benefit while we were there and we'd pool it together to buy our groceries. Not much would be left over after the supermarket shop each week — sometimes there'd be enough to go for a day trip to some local pools. We'd arrive on a bus and each be handed about $2.50 in spending money, like a bunch of kids. It must have looked like such a crack-up. It was the first place I really learned how to budget.

The Woolshed programme was therapy-based, so there was a lot of time for group discussions and introspection, super-intense. When I turned up I didn't know it was routine for the group to be told about each new arrival before they got there. So when everyone knew my name I freaked out, convinced they were all cops. I was only two weeks clean, and I was on edge and paranoid. The first couple of days I sat in the groups in complete silence, not saying a damn word.

That silence, though, was only on the outside. Inside, the noise was at full volume, bouncing around my brain. At night I had insomnia and could only sleep for about two hours, and then I'd wake up, reliving everything that had happened to me. In the group sessions, I couldn't listen to the others because all I could hear were the voices in my head repeating to me the lines I'd been fed for so many years: *You're a piece of fucking shit. You're so full of shit.* On and on. And as if that wasn't enough, scenes of my past trauma would start playing out, incidents repeating and repeating over and over. The trauma, the abuse, the self-hate, on a loop. It was unbearable.

Earlier in my life, drugs had provided an escape but didn't solve the problem. Rehab showed me that my problems were manageable without substance abuse and gave me tools to deal with them. Because eventually, slowly but surely, others' words began to seep in. I started realising that other people were saying some of the things I was thinking. Not exactly the same, but something similar — why they used drugs, the desperation they felt. I could relate. And some of them talked about the abuse they'd had at home, and of course I could relate to that, too. I heard aspects and fragments of my own story, my own thoughts.

I started opening up. Initially that might not have been apparent to anyone else, since I wasn't saying much. But I was being present, truly present in the groups, and really listening and taking on what the others were saying. Then, word by nervous word, I started talking about me. It was the first time I'd ever done it, in all my 23 years: this is what happened to me; this is how I feel.

In the beginning, my efforts would be halting. After a few sentences, I'd be telling myself: *That's enough. Shut up.* But then it started to flow out of me. And it was like a release. I started to understand why I did some of the shit I did. I could see the reasons for where I was in life, how I'd ended up here. I started making connections, drawing the dots between my drug use and my mental health and what I'd endured. I started to experience me and understand me. And it was fucking beautiful.

I'd done it by telling the truth. That instinct I'd honed over years to bullshit, bullshit, bullshit . . . to lie and avoid and obfuscate — a skill which had served me so well for so long — I felt myself being unshackled from it. I could see the only way to break free was to speak the truth, as painful and ugly as it was. I needed to get it out. This was the only place that I ever got to be vulnerable, to bawl my eyes out, to crack open the tough shell that had encased that scared little kid for all those years. I distinctly remember the first time I went an entire day without any self-deprecating thoughts, without thinking I was useless. It was the first time in about seventeen years, and it was amazing.

After a while there were fewer tears. They got replaced by an intense focus, and new thoughts: *Yes, I'm on the right path. Yes, I need to do this. Yes, I can do this.* I grabbed at every suggestion the counsellors made. I became consumed by an intense desire for honesty, not just for myself but for others, too. I was fixated on the idea of becoming well and helping others become well, too, and keeping them on the straight and narrow.

There was a guy in our cabin who would get up at night and take food from the fridge. The thing was, any leftovers were for sharing the next day; and given the budget we were on, to my mind he was being dishonest when we were all trying to be honest there. I'd become hell-bent on that, to the extent I needed to call things out no matter what. It was such a radical shift from where I'd once been. Previously, when I saw bullshit I'd often just zip my lips. Like that meeting at home when the cops came around to see my mum and stepfather. I could have spoken up, but I chose to say nothing. Or other times when I was with the boys on the streets and I'd notice something that shouldn't be happening or wasn't right: I wouldn't speak up, even though I knew it was wrong. It just wasn't what you did.

And yet, here I was giving the hard word to some guy in my cabin who was probably just a bit hungry, like I was some paragon of honesty and he'd committed some massive crime. 'You're fucking up,' I told him. 'This needs to stop. I'm not trying to be a prick here; I'm trying to help you.'

I was single-minded about standing up for the truth. So much so, it ended in me feeling I had no choice but to leave.

It was over a woman. I was with her in one of the cabins and it became apparent we could have sex. I didn't say no, but I just let it slide, paying no attention to it. But because of my new-found 'honesty at all costs' approach, I brought it up with someone else. And because *he* was trying to be super-honest as well, a culture of no secrets, he brought it up at a meeting in front of the woman. She straight out denied it.

Maybe it was a misunderstanding (not to my mind); maybe she just didn't want to have it brought up in a group — who knows? But immediately, it stung me, hard. *Fuck this shit*, I thought. For so many years I'd survived by adopting a code. A code of my own when I was growing up, a code when I was living the streets, and a code when I was in the gang. At that exact moment, it was like the new code I was developing had been broken. A line had been crossed that I couldn't ignore. It hurt that I was being honest and she was lying.

I decided the only thing I could do was leave. I'd been there for a few months and it had made such a difference to me, helping me see things I had not been able to before, and silencing the internal noise. I didn't want to go backwards, but I couldn't stay there, either.

There was a path ahead of me, but I didn't know where it was going to take me.

Chapter 9

The Accidental Businessman

Going to The Woolshed had helped me understand things about myself and make a connection between my drug use and the abuse I'd suffered as a child. It had helped me be vulnerable for the first time in my life. But my decision to leave, coming from my dogmatic commitment to honesty, meant I was on my own again, away from the support I'd had for the previous few months.

The first problem was I had nowhere to live. Luckily I found a Kiwi — there's always one somewhere, right? — who was working for the South Australian state housing department, and she was able to get me a little unit in one of the Adelaide suburbs, Norwood. So there I was parked up in the unit, living off the sickness benefit, knowing that I needed to keep progressing with my sobriety. I turned to Narcotics Anonymous (NA), and would go to meetings twice a day, walking there and back for the day meeting and the night meeting. I just needed that support, to be around others in my position, to keep focused on my recovery, to stay clean.

And it was great in that regard. It also helped me become more articulate. In the beginning I was still so new at expressing what I was feeling that I'd stumble over my words and feel stink, and just end up sitting down. But in that environment I felt comfortable and I grew in confidence.

I decided I should start being of service, so I became the secretary of a meeting for people who were newly clean, called Absolute Beginners. Part of the reason I did it was also that The Woolshed used to send a bus full of residents down to it, so it was good to see them and to give back. The meetings were on a Friday night which, when you're trying to get clean, is one of the most dangerous times of the week. As secretary I'd be the first one there, turn off the alarms in the building, set up the chairs and cups of tea, and then start the meeting off by calling up the speakers.

I became efficient and good at the job, and it continued to help me improve at standing up and speaking. It became much easier to articulate my feelings rather than letting things gnaw away or finding ways to blank them out. Having a routine was extremely helpful, too. Going to NA meetings twice a day, Absolute Beginners on a Friday, week after week after week. In fact, that's the way it was for two years.

Eventually, I realised I needed to progress. I wanted to stay clean, but I also wanted to move on with my life. To do something — but what?

At the daytime NA meetings I saw people who would come in during their lunchbreaks from work, and I thought, *Yeah, I could do that. Keep clean but find a job.* It wasn't like that moment looking out of the prison window at the blue sky, or when I had a similar realisation living in the crack house. But once again there was that drive, that desire, to look for something else.

I'd started playing in a local rugby league competition. It was good to be playing sport and socialising with others, although I wasn't exactly fit. I'd put on what they call the 'rehab spread' — when you go clean, most people tend to put on a bit of weight. I certainly had. But I enjoyed getting out on the field and running around. One day we were playing against a guy I knew who worked in security, so I asked him if there were any jobs going.

'Maybe,' he said, 'but there's two things — you'll have to go and see the boss, and you're going to have to start playing for us.'

The next week, I'd changed clubs and I'd gone to the security firm boss, a part-Māori, part-Fijian guy who ran a taekwondo gym. He had a bit of a test for me, to see if I was up to the job. 'Let's see how you go against these guys,' he said, and pointed to a couple of black belts.

For the past two years I'd been doing yoga and meditation, not even thinking about violence let alone getting into any fights. But obviously the aggression and fight-craft weren't far beneath the surface. The first guy threw a spinning kick in my direction and I caught his leg and biffed him to the ground. The next guy was a bit more conservative but I smashed him as well.

The boss was happy and said he could get me some work. But first, he said, I'd need to sort out the rehab spread and get fit. There was a weights room and punching bags, so I started going there regularly, working up a sweat and getting used to using my fists again. With the rugby league as well, I got real fit real quick.

+ + +

Soon enough, I was working in bars and clubs. Initially I was extremely placid, the most polite bouncer you'd ever meet. My first roles were inside the bars; people would be playing up or smoking on the dance floor and I'd be asking them to stop, being real nice about it. But things changed one night.

A bunch of guys turned up and tried to force their way into the bar. I went to the front door to help — there were about four of us and about eight of them. Things were really kicking off when suddenly something inside me snapped and I went crazy. At the end of it, as the sound of ambulance and police sirens got nearer, all the other guys were shaking their heads and saying, 'What happened?' I just said, 'Oh, it's a long story . . .' and turned and went back inside to carry on working.

That inner rage, that instinct to fight or die — it was still there inside me. The difference was now I could control it. And with no drugs (or booze) in my system, there was nothing to soften that control, either. I became super-clinical with my fury. I'd never hit anyone unless they started to get aggressive. But as soon as they took a swing, that was it: I'd put them out. And I'd do it in front of everyone so there was a clear message for all in the vicinity: 'Don't fuck with me.'

The company got a reputation: whichever clubs or pubs we were in, no one would play up. It meant we ended up getting called up to go and sort out the worst places, pubs that were overrun. We got involved in some massive brawls, but we always came out on the right side.

One night we were in a pub where there was a live band playing, a bogan band. And half the bogans in Adelaide turned up to party. Everyone was drinking pretty heavily and having a good night. After the band finished, a guy in the crowd started playing up, getting all stroppy. I told him he needed to leave — nicely, of course — and he tried to step me out. Well, that meant I couldn't be nice anymore, could I? There were about 200 bogans watching. I smacked the guy to the ground and started dragging him towards the door.

For some reason, he started getting heavier and heavier. I looked around and there was another guy clinging on to the guy's leg. Then another one, then another one. It was a chain of bogans. I got them all outside, and by then the crowd had got agitated. About 40 of them gathered outside and surrounded us, me and about five of my colleagues. It was on. We just backed up to the door and refused to give in, absolutely going for it. By the end there were about two dozen bogans on the ground and the rest had run away.

It only added to our reputation. Things were generally quiet if we were around. Bikies would come up to us and shake our hands and ask if it was okay for them to come in. 'Yeah, cool, come in,' we'd say. Bikie clubs were a big thing in Adelaide at that time, in the 1990s. Certain pubs and nightclubs would be known to be connected to the patch of one club, so the others would stay away. If there was trouble, the pub managers knew we could sort it out. Like one time, two clubs were having a feud and about 50 of one club turned up at a pub which was known to be the patch of their rivals. The manager rang us up, and about twelve of us went down. The group respected us being outnumbered but still having the heart to turn up. The other club guys didn't show, so they left, and the manager and pub owner fucking loved us.

We were all earning good money — especially the boss, who bought about five or six houses on his street with the profits. As well as working the clubs, he had us doing security in malls during the day, so there was plenty of work. I was fit, and I was still clean. If I went out for a drink with the guys after work, I'd be sipping on milk — I didn't even drink soft drinks in those days.

So, things were going well. Also, as a muscly young guy working in clubs all the time — yeah, there was a lot of sex. Of course I tried to be very professional about it and not mix work with pleasure; if I met a woman, I'd arrange to catch up with her after work at another club or bar or take her home. But occasionally things just happened when they happened. Sometimes the moment takes you, if you know what I mean?

\+ + +

With regular, well-paid work, the security gig was giving me a chance to enjoy life a bit. But things were about to fall apart. It was pretty much inevitable.

With the notoriety we had, power went to people's heads. Why are humans always like that? The whole situation ended up being corrosive and corrupted. Guys started doing side deals and acting like dickheads, and it got to the point where we were just as bad as everyone else. In fact, things got so bad that three guys almost got killed because of the stupidity of our boss. He was walking around town like he was the Godfather, drinking too much and thinking he owned the town. This particular night, he'd gone out with these three, all partying and carrying on. They were at a nightclub and the boss started slapping people around, getting out of hand. It was stupid, and just showed how a sense of invincibility had taken him over. That night proved how wrong that sense was.

Some other guys at the club did not take kindly to the way the boss and the boys were behaving, so they lashed out at the three boys' heads with hammers. They got fucking smashed, and damn near died — they were in hospital for months. Meanwhile the boss, who'd been acting like a fuckwit for ages now and who had caused it, *he* got away unharmed.

Until that point, I'd been loyal to the boss and to our group. One hundred per cent. But visiting those boys in hospital, I saw what a mess it had all become. It was like I could see the cancer within the group. The boss didn't even seem to care about what had happened to the guys — because of him — and so it caused a lot of bitterness in the group, too. I was disenchanted and knew it was time to get away. I didn't want to be there anymore.

Around that time, there was a little bar up in the Adelaide Hills that we used to look after. It had been having trouble with local idiots, so the owner had asked us to help clean it up. A small bar in the hills, shouldn't be a problem, right? We sent one guy up there on his own. But the local little shits jumped him. So the next night, three of us went up there and we sorted it. Put it this way: there was no more trouble at that bar. The owner loved us.

I'd been looking after this bar for months, standing there in a suit at the door — it was quite an affluent area — greeting people arriving and keeping things under control. But after the incident with the hammers, I was disillusioned. I told the bar owner what I was feeling and that I was going to leave. He said: 'I don't want to lose you. What if we take you on as our own security?'

Initially I didn't want to do that to the boss and the other guys; it made me feel disloyal. But I told the bar owner I'd think about it. I went home and pondered it over for the next few days. I wanted to leave, but if I stopped working for the boss, then what was I going to do for work? The answer seemed obvious, and it lay in the Adelaide Hills. I'd picked up all these skills working in the bars; why not use them? *Yeah, fuck it*, I thought, *I'm gonna do it*. So I told the bar owner I was in — and just like that I had my first premises to look after.

After a little while the owner introduced me to a mate of his who had another bar further south and who was keen for me to help him out, too. And then I started going out with a woman whose father owned a pub, and *he* asked me to work for him as well. Without really trying, I was building a business. After the incident with the hammers, others had been disillusioned with my former boss as well, so I had plenty of guys who wanted to come and work for me because they respected me. Soon enough, I had my own crew.

It was a proud moment. Having left New Zealand for Australia with no clue what I was going to do, then escaping the spiral of trouble and strife I was being sucked into, narrowly avoiding becoming a junkie and then going through rehab to get myself clean, I was in business. And it was a business I could run with my own values, my own code: I treated it like a brotherhood, looking after the guys properly, paying them well.

Inadvertently, I'd timed things right, too.

+ + +

In Adelaide in the late 1990s, a war broke out between bikie clubs. A new group had decided they wanted to move into the city, so the others all got together to try to stop them. It was a wild time. Violence everywhere you looked, shootings and beatings and menace. It was in the news every day, with sensational headlines and breathless news bulletins about the latest confrontation or drive-by shooting. Without sounding mercenary about it, though, it was good for business. Bar and pub owners wanted protection, and my crew and I were an unyielding shield against whatever would come to the door.

I got approached by one of the ethnic community groups; they had a bar-restaurant where they'd all get together, and they wanted me to come and keep it safe. I knew that lots of guys from this community were in bike clubs, but I agreed and started working there with my crew. One night, it was all quiet when a guy I used to work with in the bars walked in with a couple of people from the community, and he was wearing a patch — a patch belonging to the rival group that was trying to muscle its way into Adelaide. It was a bold, inflammatory move, bound to piss off people in other clubs. I knew the news would spread fast. *Ah, fuck*, I thought. *Now it's just going to go off in here. In half an hour there's going to be shots through the fucking window.*

I didn't want these guys in the bar, but I didn't want to disrespect them, either. So, while they were sitting at a table with their drinks, I grabbed some food for them, put it down, and sat down with them. We started talking, reminiscing about our days working together, having a laugh. Then I said: 'No disrespect, but how long are you going to be here? Because it would be a good night if bullets didn't come through the window.'

One of the other guys looked straight at me and said: 'Are you scared or something?' I turned to him and replied, 'If you want to find out, let's go outside right now and you can find out how stupid that question was and how fucking unlucky you are.' It's fair to say that things were tense. Then the guy I used to work with cracked up laughing, and he said to his mate: 'Remember the guy I was telling you about? That's him. Just shut up.' I guess you could say my reputation preceded me, and it was proving useful.

This was a point in my life where I was exceptionally good at violence. But it was all for a purpose. I wasn't reckless. I wasn't mindless. It was all in the line of duty. But I was dangerous, and people knew it. The three of them finished their food, downed their drinks and headed for the door. The guy I used to work with said goodbye on the way out. 'Hey, when are you going to see us and come throw on one of these?' He meant the patch. I said: 'Nah, bro. Probably not.'

Why would I go back into a gang? I'd been there, done that, and left that life behind me. Also, my business was going well — things were really taking off, my crew and I were providing security for even more places around the city, including a top strip club and a three-level nightclub. Life was good.

But then, if I've learned one thing in life, it's that you never know what's going to happen next; how the echoes of the past can sound once more.

Chapter 10

A Father's Embrace

The more time I spent in Adelaide, the more I realised how different it was. It was certainly far away from sleepy, beachside Matatā where I'd had my start in life, and from bristling, bustling Māngere where I'd spent most of my childhood — if you could call it that.

But I was feeling settled in this South Australian city. My security business was booming, I was drug- and alcohol-free, I had a girlfriend (the one whose father had a pub) — life was good. It was the late 1990s, and the pub scene was still bustling despite the bikie war. There was plenty of mahi. I had guys working for me who I trusted, and we were doing a good job, continuing to build a decent reputation. I was making good money and paying the boys well.

And then things took a turn. A sharp one.

It started with my relationship. My girlfriend was awesome, even though her dad was a bit racist and wasn't particularly impressed that his daughter was going out with a Māori boy (though he was happy to have me and my crew on the door at his premises). But I ended up sabotaging things because I still didn't know how to have a healthy relationship.

I'd done a lot of work on myself after learning how to open up at The Woolshed, getting clean and recognising the connection between getting wasted and what I'd been through. I'd had an opportunity, for the first time in my life, to look at what I'd been through, to be honest about my life and to reflect on everything. But reflection doesn't always mean resolution, and there was stuff I still hadn't confronted.

Growing up with violence, sexual abuse and psychological warfare meant I found it hard to trust anyone — let alone connect with them. Even though I was now in my early thirties it was a demon I could not shake, a demon that haunted me and hurled curveballs at my mental state. With my girlfriend, I'd just go quiet sometimes. She couldn't understand why, and at the time, neither did I. There were times I didn't even know I'd gone quiet.

In fact I was depressed, but I didn't have the language, didn't have the comprehension, didn't understand that I was in my own head and messed up about stuff. And in those days people still weren't talking openly about mental health and depression like we do today. My girlfriend didn't know why I couldn't talk about what I was feeling. I never messed around on her — loyalty was always critical for me — but I was not decent boyfriend material. And so she left me. Who could blame her?

While that wasn't great, there was still so much going on in my life, and I'd made so much progress, that by rights I should have been able to work through it. The sensible thing would have been to take a pause on relationships, at least until I'd got some help or figured out how to stare down that demon. Instead, on the rebound, I ended up in a relationship with another woman. At the time I thought, *Yeah, this is what I want*. And the reason I thought that way? She was just as broken as I was, and we had similar backgrounds.

From the start, it was bedlam. She was fantastically smart, but we were extremely toxic together. I spiralled out of control very quickly. Within a month of meeting her, I was back drinking again. Hard out. And within two months, I was back on drugs — two months of being in that relationship had undone all the gains I'd made in the past few years, reversed all the steps I'd taken.

And then — three months after we hooked up — she was pregnant. It may not have been the best of relationships but, honestly, I was excited. I wanted to be a dad. But from the get-go, her pregnancy became another tool she'd use to manipulate me.

My work in the clubs and pubs became a problem for her. 'Oh, no, you're not working in the clubs tonight — you need to do this, you need to do that,' she'd say. And because I wanted things to work, for the sake of our baby, I would listen to her. But with each manipulation, with each toxic twist, I became more and more fucked up again. I was back to being a heavy-drinking, drugged-up mess.

Except there was a baby on the way, which did make me happy. I was getting ready, trying to find the way back to a straight pathway. I bought us a house with a white picket fence. We got married. I was driving around in a brand-new Ford Falcon with plenty of space in the back for a baby's car seat. On the surface, at least, I was on the trajectory of settling down and being part of a family. Suburban bliss.

When it came time for the baby to arrive, we went to hospital. She was yelling and screaming, and I got the impression the staff were a bit scared. A nurse came into the room and my partner told her: 'I want this baby *out*.' The nurse was on one side of her with my partner's heel pushing into her hip, and she told me to get on the other side and do the same, like a couple of human stirrups. My partner pushed and screamed, the baby's head started to appear, then it would go back in, then in, then out. I'd never been around a birth so I had no idea what was happening.

And then, magic — the baby came out and flopped into my hands. A boy. My precious boy. He was so beautiful. But he wasn't breathing. I was terrified. The nurse took him, and another staff member came in, and they helped him.

And finally, we heard him cry. I was ecstatic. It meant the world to me. I kissed him on the head.

My whole life, I'd been searching for my own dad, even though I knew virtually nothing about him. In those moments of fear when I was a child, I'd pleaded for my dad to come and find me. My whole life, I'd wanted my dad to love me, to hug me. Instead, as a six-year-old I'd been introduced to a man who took the place of a father in my life, and who acted nothing like that for eight years — hitting me, kicking me, punching me and yelling at me. My whole life, I'd wanted to feel that unconditional love of a father for their son. I never thought I would.

But finally, here it was. When my son was a little bit older, and he ran and threw himself at me, wrapping his little arms as far around me as he could, squeezing tight and squishing his face into me, I knew this was what I'd wanted all along. This was the feeling I'd missed and longed for. My heart was full, the dad-sized hole plugged by this small human, my boy.

I knew he was destined for big things, my boy. He was not even 24 hours old, and he was looking at me when I held my finger up in front of his eyes. I moved my finger from side to side, up and down, and he tracked it with his eyes. He was so smart, like he'd been here before.

+ + +

Once he came home from hospital, my life revolved around my boy. When I was home, I was with him 100%. When I was working, it was to earn what I could for him so he could have the best of everything. It was all about him.

Meanwhile, his mother was using him to manipulate me. And it worked. She had me twisted around her little finger, and as a consequence I got wound up. It got volatile. She would hit me. Most times, she'd bash me in the face and I'd turn and walk out. But one time, and I am not proud of this, she had me cornered and she was hitting me and I lashed back. Immediately after it happened, I regretted it.

'What'd you do that for? You fucking bastard, you hit me!'

She left, and she took my son.

I was devastated, both for losing my son and for losing my shit. After all I'd been through. It sent me into an absolute tailspin of depression. I was on the verge of a mental breakdown, alone once more, and now no longer living with the boy I loved with all my heart.

I wanted to be with him all the time, but that was not an option. Instead, any opportunity to spend time with him was the one thing that kept me going. I'd steal moments with him when his mother wanted to go out partying. In fact, I'd give her money to go out so I could be alone with my boy. I cherished every second. But it only amplified the loneliness and pain I felt when I wasn't with him. I'd drink. I'd do drugs. I'd retreat into my suffering. I was back where I'd been before, a dangerous place for me to be.

Right about then, my son's mother filed for divorce, which I was relieved about — she rang me up and said: 'I know you're upset, but don't think about killing yourself. Don't try it.'

What the fuck? Was she trying to plant the seed? I couldn't believe it. If that was the plan, though, luckily it didn't work. Although it didn't help pull me out of the dark place I'd landed, either. I started gambling. I started putting on weight — a shitload of weight; I was obese. I also started running my business into the ground. I fell behind with the taxes, and I took my eye off the ball. Everything I'd created was falling apart. I was forced into a position I didn't want to be in. I ended up having to sell the house I'd bought for our future, for the family which had been destroyed. I also had to sell my business.

Within two years of meeting my ex, I'd lost my business, my house, my self-esteem, my sobriety. So many of the things I'd worked so, so hard for were now gone. Stewing in this state, I couldn't see a future. And I started to wonder if all the things I'd done to make myself better, to improve my life, were worth it. *What's the fucking point? Why keep striving to do things when I can just lose it all?*

And then another thought, one seeded in my past, occurred to me: *Maybe all I'm destined for is to be a gangster.*

+ + +

By that time, I'd met up with a Māori boy who had joined the new bikie club in town, the one that had decided to muscle its way into Adelaide. Things had moved on: the war was over, and in the truce that followed it was agreed that the outsiders would be allowed to stay. Of course there was still some animosity, but the full-on fights and shootings had finished, leaving an uneasy peace.

And I ended up joining the new arrivals.

I wasn't clean of drugs, but I wasn't the same mess I was after the break-up with my ex. And because of my reputation — or maybe you could call it notoriety — from when I worked in security, they snapped me up. I skipped being a prospect and got a patch straight away, as well as a rank — a rank that meant I had seniority in times of conflict. It was a recognition of my past propensity for violence.

Gangs in Australia were very different from New Zealand.

There were still internal politics at play, just like at home, but it was like that was on steroids. It was because the benefits were astonishing — there was so much money at stake. At home, joining a group was more about the ideology, the whanaungatanga; remember how most members at home were drawn from poor backgrounds, and being together gave a sense of identity and togetherness? In Australia it was much, much more about the money. Becoming a member was like joining a business. The financial rewards on offer were staggering.

If you think of it in business terms, I was in management. It meant I got to sit at tables few people sat at. I got to see how decisions were made and observe some extremely intelligent people. They were experts at utilising what they had to make more money and manoeuvring the assets they had to create maximum intimidation. But it wasn't just muscle for the sake of muscle; it was all about increasing your power, increasing your ability to expand and, ultimately, increasing your wealth.

Being at the top table honed a skill I'd first picked up many years ago. I prided myself on being able to read a situation; to listen to what people were saying and to figure out what they actually meant. Because sometimes words did not match intentions. In the new environment I'd moved into, sometimes it seemed like there was a game of high-stakes poker on the go. Who was bluffing? Who was sitting on something but saying nothing? I became very adept at being part of conversations where I would be listening, but at the same time in my head I'd be operating at another level translating what it all meant. In the back of my mind I'd be thinking: *What's really going on here? What's going to happen?* It was a handy skill to have — one that would save me later on.

+ + +

With the truce in place, the patch on my back and a seat at the top table, I was able to start making moves quickly. Because I had the position and the authority, I could put things in place rapidly to start making serious money.

Normally, a boss in a power dynamic like that would pocket a significant chunk but give enough to the underlings that they would be hungry for more and keep coming back. It's the capitalist way, right? But I guess you could call me the socialist gangster, the outlaw Karl Marx. I was more interested in distributing the wealth. My theory was that operating in a more inclusive, share-the-wealth way was good for growth, too. The best way to rise was for us all to rise. By doing that, we could spread further and quicker.

I'd gone into this world mostly because I didn't know what else to do with my life, rather than because I wanted to be a committed member. But I knew I was good at it, and I knew I could make it work. I had the skills, the smarts and the notoriety.

I had big ideas, not just for myself and the club, but also for the community where I was based. I ran a tight, disciplined operation, insisting that the suburb we were in was safe for everyone. And it worked — no old ladies getting mugged, no sexual assaults in the streets. It felt good to be having some positive influence, albeit against the backdrop of building a criminal enterprise.

Now the threat of gang warfare had diminished, all we had to do was get on with making money; all we had to do was trust each other and keep the faith — and watch out for law enforcement, of course. Simple. And the way things were going, we were on the verge of it being a fucking gold mine.

But then I started to notice things. Nothing you could put a finger on, exactly. It wasn't what was being said; it was much more subtle than that. Those skills I'd developed to pick up what was actually going on? They were about to come in real handy. Because if I didn't act, my world was about to come crashing down around me. Big time.

Chapter 11

Danger All Around

The first real sign of trouble, the first time my senses really told me something was up, arrived with a dish of fettuccine marinara. There was an Italian restaurant in Adelaide I enjoyed going to. The owner liked us coming there because we'd spend a shitload of money, and while we were there he also felt protected. So we'd always get looked after.

I was with another guy from the club, sitting in our usual place — a table in the corner where the lighting was low, and away from other patrons so we could talk without being listened to. He was patched but didn't hold a position like I did, so was lower ranked than me. I was tucking into my marinara (that was always my go-to dish, but they also did a mean carbonara) and we were laughing and joking. Good times.

Then, out of the blue, he asked me if I could move some guns for him. Of course, even though we were out of other people's earshot, the request came in coded language. You could never be too careful. But it was clear what he meant.

'I've got an aunty upstate who came down to visit me and she brought all these clothes with her, and she left them behind and I need to send them back to her,' he said. He had his arms folded, and he was tapping one arm with two fingers from the opposite hand in a shape like a pistol.

'There's a whole shitload of clothes and I don't want to pay for a moving van to shift them. So could you shift them for me?' In case it's not obvious, 'clothes' meant guns.

I had a smile fixed on my face, and I nodded: 'Yeah, yeah. We could do that.' But in the back of my mind I was thinking: *What the fuck is going on here?* This was the first time he'd ever asked me to do anything like that. And it was not the way things were done. But I kept my suspicions well hidden. 'Sure, mate. We can work something out,' I said, jabbing my fork into the bowl of pasta.

Meanwhile, I was quickly processing what was happening here, figuring out why he would do such an unusual thing. That ability to take part in a conversation while also sitting back and deciphering its true meaning was working overtime. And then I clicked. Or at least I had a strong idea, partly due to an earlier strange conversation with this same guy.

\+ + +

Around this time, the Australian Federal Police, as well as the state police and other law-enforcement agencies, were targeting organised crime in a concerted way. It was not long after the 9/11 terror attacks on America in 2001, and the government was using them as an opportunity to usher in all sorts of new laws and measures. It was a parliamentary frenzy — one academic calculated that between the 2001 attacks and late 2007, a new anti-terror law was introduced in Australia on average every seven weeks.

Even though, supposedly, these laws didn't specifically target motorcycle gangs, the government's reasoning was that organised crime groups had networks to move things around the country — which was true, as I very well knew — and so they justified the crackdown by saying they were cutting off opportunities for terrorist organisations. To undermine those networks they needed to tap inside them, to infiltrate the gangs.

This was what I believed was behind that earlier suspicious conversation with the guy at the restaurant. He'd started talking to me about how it would be useful to have law enforcement on our side. 'Let's get some of them working for us,' he said. On the face of it, this was a smart idea. Corrupt cops can certainly help smooth the way, as decades of Australian criminal history has shown. Once upon a time the country had so many bent cops, the joke was that Australia had the best police force money could buy. So the strategy he was floating — with cops on the take, prepared to turn a blind eye or better still smooth the way, we could expand even more rapidly — was solid.

But you only had to look at what was happening in society at the time to know this was not the time for it. Right in the middle of a crackdown? Nah, bro. So why did he say that? I started to wonder if he was being naïve, or stupid, or if he was being manipulated, being used as some sort of double agent. I didn't know. So I played it straight, rejecting his idea outright. 'No, we're not doing that,' I told him.

'Okay, fair enough,' he replied.

If it was just a naïve idea, that would have been the end of it. But then all these other things started happening — like his request that I suddenly become an interstate gunrunner. During a crackdown on terrorism? What the fuck?

+ + +

I was still sitting on my suspicions about this guy, trying to figure out what he was up to, when other shit started to happen. It was like those old kung fu movies where it's not just one assailant who comes at you — they come in a pack, and when one falls the next one steps into the fray.

As if to confirm that I was being targeted, a weird thing happened. It involved a Māori boy I'd done a bit of work with. One night he was at a pub in the middle of nowhere, out the back of beyond, when he absolutely smashed someone — pummelled him to the point where an emergency chopper had to be called to collect the guy. He very nearly killed him; it was a huge deal, and the cops were on the case. But — four weeks later, he was still walking around, scot-free. No one could figure out how he hadn't been locked up. It was a bit strange.

Around that time, this guy got hold of me and said: 'Hey, Tim. Can we catch up?'

'Sweet, bro. When?' He said he had a bit on, and would it be alright if we met at a notorious bar at three in the morning? I was pretty used to doing business at that time of day, and of course I'd done a bit of business with this guy, so I agreed. Bit odd, but okay.

Not long before the meeting, he rang again. 'Hey, Tim, are you still coming?'

'Course, bro. See you there.' Again, I thought: *Bit odd, but fair enough.*

I walked into the bar we were meeting at, grabbed a drink and headed for the pokie machines. I was wearing a top with the name of my club on it, so it wouldn't have been a good idea to just sit in the bar itself; better to tuck around the corner with the pokies. It was routine to do that when you were having these kinds of meetings because it didn't pay to be too obvious.

Having said that, I did have an ulterior motive too. I was addicted to gambling. Big time. I'd truly picked up a bunch of bad habits — being back on the drugs was only one of them. I was smoking a lot of ice. And mad, mad gambling.

So there I was, playing the pokies, wasting the time away as well as my money. And the guy wasn't turning up. I looked at the time: three o'clock came and went. *Hmmmm. Oh, well.* More money went in the slot, and time ticked on. I looked at the time again: four o'clock now. *Where the fuck is he?*

Just then, a bunch of other guys walked in, all from one of the other clubs.

I'd been fucking set up.

I stood up, and recognised one of the guys I used to work on the doors with. We always got on, but he was with another club now. There were also some young guys who looked like they were straining at the leash, keen to have a go at me. 'Man, they want to eat you,' said the guy I knew.

'It will be a fucking tough meal, I tell you that much,' I replied.

I was outnumbered and vulnerable. But I was not afraid. 'We can do this if you want,' I told him. 'I don't give a fuck. But take this as gospel: if we start this today, you're gonna be in this situation tomorrow. Just think about that.' In other words, whatever these guys started here was going to end elsewhere. And it wouldn't be pretty.

He thought about what I'd said, and he must have had second thoughts. But in this world, saving face was a big deal. So he needed a compromise. His group did a bit of work on this street, so they had a reputation to protect. They couldn't risk anyone finding out that I'd come into their 'hood wearing an emblem from a rival club and had got away with it.

'Okay, what should we do about that?' I asked him.

'If you leave now and make it look like we made you leave, we keep face.'

I could have stayed for the fight — I did love a fight, after all. But I knew I had a bigger problem on my hands that I needed to deal with. So I got out of the bar, making it look like I'd been shifted on, and I started to plot what I was going to do about the Māori boy who had betrayed me. I couldn't help but think he'd done it because law enforcement had made him. Was he working for them now? It was the only explanation I could come up with for why he wasn't in prison for smashing that guy to within an inch of his life.

I tried to get hold of him on the phone, but he wouldn't pick up. I cast my net elsewhere. There was this young guy who used to hang out with him who was now in another club. With the help of some guys in my club, we arranged to meet this friend. He came along with some senior members from his club. We all turned up without wearing patches, because if things popped off it would get very complicated — meetings like this were politically hot. If things did unfold, at least I could say to my higher-ups that I wasn't wearing my patch.

Anyway, this young guy was sitting there with the senior members and he was shitting himself. 'Where's your mate?' I asked him.

'I don't know.' Clearly it was a lie; the guy was probably parked just down the road waiting for an update.

'Well, I need to have a chat with him because he set me up and we have a lot to discuss. You'd better tell him to get in touch with me because the next time I see you, if I haven't spoken to your mate then you and I won't be chatting.'

I stood up, shook hands with the senior member of the other gang, and left.

As soon as the meeting was over, the hierarchy of both clubs were on the phone to each other. People weren't happy the meeting had happened. But because I'd not worn my patch, nothing could be done about it, especially because I held a rank. I'd gone about things by the book.

There was still a problem to be dealt with, however — the

guy who had set me up. And that would only be the start of it. By now, I'd started to make the connection to that thing that had happened: the question about moving guns interstate. I could see everything that was in play, like pieces on a chessboard. I knew that if I wanted, I could have a good go at taking out those who were causing me problems, or at least die trying. I wasn't afraid of anything.

I thought hard about my situation. I had a choice: risk it all and be the gangster I knew I could be — or go home, back to New Zealand.

+ + +

When I joined up, I was not fully committed. Jumping into the club and taking the patch was an ego boost; probably one I needed at the time. Going straight to being a patched member and getting the rank had made me feel good. Sitting around the table with those smart guys making big decisions was impressive.

Coming from the low point I was at, it helped drag me back up. I'd learned so much — about taking in the wider picture, about understanding and calculating risks. But in the back of my head, I knew this life wasn't for me. And now things were in a precarious position. It was time to move on. Being a gangster was not for me anymore.

In the end, it was a straightforward decision: I was going to leave and go home. However, that was easier said than done. You don't just hand in your resignation, collect your final payslip and jump on the plane. Especially when you are pretty sure there's a target on your back.

Complicating matters was the fact that I was taking a lot of drugs, especially ice. I was nearly going psychotic on them, especially when I thought about all the shit that was going down. I wasn't sleeping, and thinking of all the scenarios that could play out made me hyperventilate. I needed to get control of myself and quickly.

Luckily, I had my son. He was still my world — always will be. He centred me and grounded me. I went around to see him and got to spend time with him on my own, chilling out. It brought me back to solid ground.

My boy was the only thing holding me in Australia, and it was going to be heartbreaking leaving him behind with his Australian mother — it would be a long time before I saw him again. But I needed to get away, keep myself alive and make a future for him in New Zealand; a place that he could come to, a place he'd never known but where he could stand one day and know it was his home. As much as it hurt, I knew this was the right decision.

Handing in my patch was going to be difficult, too. As the new club in Adelaide, there weren't a lot of our patches in town. If I just passed my patch over, it would have been easy for the people who wanted to take me out to set me up: get another brown boy to wear my patch and cause some trouble. And then point the finger at me: 'Yeah, there was a dark-skinned guy in a patch there.' Suddenly, I'd be carrying the shit for something I didn't do and every cop in the state would be on the lookout for me. Instead, I kept the patch until the last minute, headed to the airport and mailed it back from there.

I was going home, to the place I'd run away from. In Australia I'd been through so much — becoming a junkie, getting clean, building and losing a business, becoming a gangster again and, most importantly, becoming a dad. I didn't know what my future held. But as the plane took off, and I looked over towards the blue sky beyond, just as I had in Waikeria Prison, I knew things did not have to be the way they had turned out.

It was time for another change.

Chapter 12

The Activist

I'd tried to plan as best I could for my arrival back in Aotearoa. Leaving Australia had been fraught, but I'd scrambled (as discreetly as I could) to make sure I had enough money to make a proper start when I got back home, a nest egg. But there were a few logistical issues that needed navigating to get the money home safely.

The last thing I wanted was any trouble, especially since the cops and border officials would be watching me closely. So I made sure I knew the rules and followed them to the letter. I didn't want to put the money in the bank; instead, I decided I'd carry it back. But you could only have $10,000 cash on you, so that's what I did, leaving a chunk behind. Then I grabbed one of my family members and we went straight back to Adelaide to collect two more lots of $10,000, one lot each.

The problem was, he was not as cautious or as astute as me. During our couple of days on the ground back in Australia he went out partying and had hardly any sleep. By the time we were due to fly home he was hyped-up and paranoid. He looked so agitated and anxious that of course he drew attention to himself at the airport; he got pulled aside as we went through Customs in Australia and was taken to a small room. All he had to do was keep calm. He wasn't doing anything wrong — I'd made sure he wasn't carrying a cent more than he was allowed. But behind that closed door, under interrogation, I wondered what would happen.

Finally, they let him go and we boarded the plane. I tried to reassure him, but now he was even more paranoid and started having hallucinations and getting all worked up. I was doing my best to keep him calm, but the law enforcement people had really got into his head. When we landed, he was still really worked up.

'It's okay,' I told him quietly, 'you've done nothing wrong and you're doing nothing wrong.' All I had to do was get him through the doors into the arrival hall in Auckland and we'd be safe, and I'd have a decent whack of that nest egg.

As we got closer to the arrivals desk, he full-on panicked, turned back and started heading the way we'd come. This was going from bad to worse. He was determined to go into the bathroom and flush the money down the toilet. I was equally determined to stop that happening. People were wondering what the fuck was happening and, no doubt, behind the mirrored glass upstairs the authorities were watching via the cameras too.

I grabbed hold of him, marched him towards the exit and basically threw him at the desk of the last border official we needed to get past. 'He's been out partying all night, don't worry about him,' I said, mustering my best 'Keep Calm and Carry On' persona, and willing the sweat to stop dripping down my face.

The guy behind the desk took our forms. He barely looked up. No doubt the Aussies had told them exactly what was going on, that there was nothing they could pin on us and there was no point wasting time on us. Because the next thing I knew we were being waved towards the door.

Even though I was sure that would be the outcome, it was a relief. It's almost the hardest I've had to work for $10,000, I reckon. I decided I'd wait a little longer to go and collect more of the money I had stashed as well as some I was owed.

+ + +

In the meantime, my plan was to head out of Auckland, earn some Kiwi dollars one way or another, and reconnect with whānau. Living in Australia, it had been years since I'd seen much of my cousins and aunties and uncles. I went to Meremere, where some family members lived, including my mum and stepfather. I'd only had limited contact with them since that stare-off with my stepfather across the table after I'd come out of prison the first time. I'd see them occasionally at whānau gatherings like tangi, but there was too much painful history for us to have much of a relationship. They were parents in name only. In Meremere now, I attempted to reconnect but it just didn't work out. The gap between us was still too big, and so much about my childhood was left unsaid.

Life in Meremere, a town on the banks of the Waikato River, famous for its drag strip and power station, had its advantages. It's a small, semi-rural township and easy to rent a house, especially when I was prepared to pay three months in advance.

I wanted to be someplace where I could keep a low profile, because I knew the cops would be keeping a close eye on me — something they'd done every time I'd come back to New Zealand for a visit. One time I was briefly home from Australia for a whānau tangi, and when I got back to Adelaide Mum rang and said: 'The police came looking for you — they say the description of that rapist on the loose looks like you.' *What?* I had no idea what she was talking about.

It turned out that the guy the cops were looking for was the serial rapist Malcolm Rewa. When he was finally caught, you could see he looked nothing like me except we both had brown skin. Rewa had been sexually attacking women for years. I had no history that would even *begin* to make me a suspect — and I hadn't even been in the country. And yet the police were putting me in the frame or, at best, wanting to rule me out. It was ridiculous. It seemed that the propensity for the cops to pounce on me for anything — even complete bullshit — remained strong.

So when I came home for good, I was naturally wary. It didn't help that I'd notice cars following me or parked in strange places; likely the cops just waiting for me to trip up. I had a stack of criminal convictions from my teenage years, and I'd been in gangs on both sides of the Tasman, so they were probably itching to throw the book at me. For my part, I just had to keep my nose clean.

+ + +

As I drove around and saw the country I'd come home to, I noticed that things hadn't improved for Māori. Since the late 1990s and into the early 2000s, there had been a lot of talk — policies like 'Closing the Gap' — but we were still at the bottom of all the social indicators. Very much so.

One thing that *had* changed was the political landscape. The Māori Party had been formed in the aftermath of the Foreshore and Seabed Act, a law change that robbed iwi of rights won in court. Outrageous. The party was still in its infancy, but it was growing in strength in the lead-up to the 2005 election. I started to go along to rallies and get involved a bit. I saw it as my opportunity to contribute — although, at the time, I was also still seeing if I could propagate an underground business empire and spread some of the wealth around; similar to impulses I'd had in Adelaide when things were going well.

I doorknocked for the party around Meremere, went to meetings in the Tainui district, and gave out flyers at flea markets. Ever the entrepreneur, I started to think of ways to raise some money for the party, as well as spirits. I had some whānau members in west Auckland who were musicians, and I helped them record a track as a bit of a theme song for the Māori Party.

It was called 'Move Forward', and it debuted on Māori Television and then got distributed to iwi radio stations. We made copies on CDs to sell for the party.

Around this time, I decided I needed to change tack, and change towns, too. I'd also realised I was going to have to give up on the rest of the money in Australia. I'd rung my boy's mother, and she told me a guy who owed me a lot of money was asking after me. 'He said he had something for you,' she told me.

In that world, such a phone call was highly unusual — in fact, under no circumstances would you go around telling people that you've got something for someone else. It was extremely suspicious. Someone was looking for me alright — but it was unlikely to be because they were desperate to repay me.

I'd have to write it all off and start again. It wasn't worth taking the risk to go and collect the money.

\+ + +

So I headed to Auckland, with no money and no place to stay. Since coming home, though, it had really hit me that I was no longer on my own. In Australia, it was mostly just me against the world. I didn't feel part of anything bigger. Here in Aotearoa, I had whānau, and I really felt connected. I didn't have two cents to rub together, but I was happy.

Some of my whānau were living in Ōrākei, on Kupe Street, and I moved in with one of my uncles to help look after him. He had end-stage COPD — chronic obstructive pulmonary disease — and was only breathing with the help of oxygen.

He needed assistance to do almost everything and I was glad to be there to help.

Kupe Street runs along a ridgeline, with shops at one end and the Ōrākei Marae at the other. The marae sits on Takaparawhau Bastion Point, the scene of one of Aotearoa's most famous Māori land protests. In the late 1970s, Māori stood up against a proposed Crown sale of the whenua. So it was appropriate that living so close to here was where my activist spirit came to life — the desire to take action to make a difference that may have first taken root when I marched to Waitangi in 1985, not really knowing what we were doing but sensing the injustice behind it.

Many of the houses in the street were state-owned, including my uncle's place. When he'd grown up, education was not a priority and so he'd left school at about eight years old, not able to read. Which made what happened next so disgraceful. Three weeks before my uncle died, after he'd moved into palliative care, a housing official turned up to see him when he was on his own. The official got him to sign a document, threatening that if he didn't sign he'd be taken to court. That document they made him sign on his deathbed saw him effectively relinquish his tenancy. And they'd done it behind the backs of the whānau.

We pushed back, trying to fight it through the Tenancy Tribunal, but didn't get a hearing date until just after we'd buried him. We tried to delay the hearing — we were still grieving — but it went ahead in our absence and we were ordered to hand the keys over and leave the house.

I couldn't believe the injustice. I thought: *I'm not leaving here, you fucking arseholes.* It wasn't that I even wanted the place: I accepted that once my uncle had died, it was going to have to revert to the state. But it was the way they handled it — the insensitivity shown to a dying man and a grieving whānau — that wound me up.

My cousin and I took it on as a mission, rallying the whole street to fight back against the government and show people they didn't have to accept being trampled on. We arranged a story in the *New Zealand Herald*, and I also called a meeting at the house and invited a bunch of politicians to come and have a cup of tea with us all; a bunch of them came, too. We got to voice our concerns in front of the politicians, and it was powerful for the people on the street and for the whānau to hear us standing up for them. It really pumped people up, and it felt good.

As the days ticked by, though, I knew the outcome wouldn't change.

We had a couple of odd things happen during that time. One was when a Pacific Island woman in her fifties knocked on the door and asked: 'Do you have any weed for sale?' It was so out of the blue. I said to her: 'I don't know who told you we did, and I don't know what you're talking about, but we don't have any weed in this house.' I suspected the cops had asked her to do it, to suss out if we were selling weed so they would have an excuse to arrest us.

Two days later, the police did turn up, not with an arrest warrant but with an eviction notice. They were acting as agents of the state in kicking us out of the home there and then. The house and others around it were demolished, but the section has just remained empty for years. What was the point of the government acting in that rushed way?

It was all over. My whānau had been moved on, and I'd had a taste of activism.

+ + +

By then, my nana was not well. She had Alzheimer's and there were times where she couldn't remember things or she'd get really confused. I went to stay with her, to help her and care for her. It was my chance to give back to this woman who had given me so much aroha and care in those first six years of my life and who had never given up believing in me.

Koro had died while I was living in Australia. So too had my younger brother, Matthew, the brother I'd first met the day my mother and stepfather picked me up from my grandparents' house; the one who I lay next to in bed, scared and confused. After our chaotic childhood and me taking to the streets, there were long periods when we didn't see each other. He had a hard, hard life, ending up in institutions where there was a lot of abuse. Not that we talked much about what happened — I had my own shit going on; and besides, it's hard to talk about that stuff. When things were going well for me in Australia, we did talk on the phone quite a bit. I told him I was sorry for being such a shit big brother, for not knowing what he'd gone through and not being there for him at the time.

'We're all good, bro,' he said. We came up with a plan for him to come over to Australia, to come and stay with me. But then he died suddenly, out of the blue.

I got back home for Matthew's tangi, but was unable to make it over for Koro's. I'd missed so much while living across the ditch. Helping Nana was a way to give back.

She was living in a state flat in Auckland CBD, 113 Greys Ave, flat 47. She had lived there for many years with Koro before he died; it was almost like going full circle. I was so grateful to be able to just sit with Nana, to laugh and share stories. It was a beautiful time. I also got to ask her where she wanted to go when the time came. 'I want to go home,' she said.

'Well, you'll go home, then, to Tapuika.'

'Thank you, boy, thank you.'

Knowing that when her days were over she'd get to return to her whenua, go back to Te Puke to lie in the embrace of her tūpuna, made her happy. And it felt good to give her that peace.

In among these good times there were distressing moments when confusion kicked in. One time she messed herself and, trying to be the independent wahine she'd always been, she tried to clean herself up but got all mixed up and flushed her knickers down the toilet. The place got a bit flooded and we had to call in the plumbers. The plumbing in that place turned out to be not so great. Soon afterwards — and this time it wasn't anything to do with Nana — the house flooded again and there was shitty water all through the place.

I rang Housing New Zealand to come and fix it, but they wouldn't — so I filmed it and got in touch with the TV news.

My experiences at Kupe Street had taught me about standing up for our whānau. After the story ran, it got cleaned up.

Because of all the trouble, though, it was decided that my nana should move out and go to live with one of my cousins instead. Big changes can be disruptive for Alzheimer's patients and impact their health. Nana went downhill quickly and died within a couple of months.

It was heartbreaking to lose this wahine toa who had stood by me and loved me and given me the best start — a start that acted like an immunisation against all that life would throw at me. While it couldn't stop the damage from happening altogether, it did provide a level of protection and shielded my inner self from being utterly destroyed. Many times I'd come close to losing everything, but it was like Nana and Koro's aroha ran so deep that I always found a way to hang on. I could never repay them, but I was determined to make them proud, determined that I had endured the worst and that there must be brightness coming.

I couldn't see that brightness yet, though. And there were to be more challenges ahead, obstacles which would crash down on me and test my spirit even more. But first, I had a job to do — to help Nana go home, just like she'd wanted.

Chapter 13

Knowing the Past, Finding the Future

Since coming back home, as well as experiencing a bit of a political awakening I'd rediscovered my Māoritanga and embraced it. My cousins had shown me the way, opening the door to reconnect me with our whakapapa and reintroduce me to tikanga. They were inspiring me to explore and to stand with pride in my culture. I signed up for te reo Māori classes at the Māngere campus of Te Wānanga o Aotearoa, and started going to our marae with my cousins. It had taken me until I was almost 40 to find my way back.

After Nana died, we took her home to her iwi, Tapuika, literally helping her return to her whenua in the urupā by her marae, Te Paamu, near Te Puke. Except, things didn't go as planned.

I was digging her grave at the urupā. We'd been told by our uncles to go six feet deep, so there I was in the hole with my shovel, digging out the earth and throwing it up to the edge. The very last shovel — the very last one! — I threw it up and I heard people screaming.

'What? What's going on there?' I called.

'Bro,' came the reply, 'you threw up a skull.' It turns out we were only supposed to go to four feet, but no one knew, so I'd accidentally disturbed one of our tūpuna.

'Oh, shit! Pass it back down to me.' But we couldn't just put it back — there was tikanga to follow. I had to sit in the grave with this skull while my cousins went to find a kaumātua. I put it down the other end and just sat there for about 40 minutes saying sorry over and over again to the skull. When the kaumātua arrived, karakia were said and things were put to right.

To fix the mistake, I had to dig into the side of the hole, away from our tūpuna. When we laid Nana to rest, we kind of had to lower her coffin down then swing her round. My cousins and I still laugh at what happened: 'Remember that skull?!'

+ + +

When I was growing up, I knew I was Māori, and I knew where Koro and Nana were from, but I didn't know my whakapapa. Understanding it and learning it, hearing the stories, is a process. It's not like you just open a book one day, or you have a chat with one of your kaumātua or kuia, and suddenly you know it all and understand it all. You learn parts, and then you learn some more, and then you put pieces together and you start to see how it all fits. It's like a giant patchwork quilt, all the generations stitched together, but at first you can't see the whole thing.

When you do, and you see where you are, you understand your place in it, your place in the world, and you can see you're part of a long, long chain. It gives you strength, it gives you purpose, it gives you a sense of identity. It's also quite mind-blowing hearing all the stories passed down through the generations, and you think, *Wow, if one thing hadn't happened by chance, I wouldn't be here . . .*

But it's not just about learning a bunch of stories, myths or legends. Learning my whakapapa would come to be incredibly important for me as I figured out some big steps in my life. It helped me understand that whatever I did, it wasn't just about me. Understanding that you descend from a long line of people who strode over your whenua and created your place in the world dissolves selfishness. It inspires you to strive for the best outcome for those who will follow *you*. You realise you're part of something much bigger than yourself.

\+ + +

When I first started going down to my marae on Koro's side, at Matatā, things were a bit bumpy for a while.

My cousins and I had heard about some marae politics we didn't agree with. There was going to be a vote about putting decision-making into the hands of a small group. We weren't having that, so we got a few of us together for the hui and drove down from Auckland in a red bus — a literal busload of us showing up! People got a bit of a surprise, and it's fair to say the hui didn't go as planned.

Things got a bit heated and someone even pulled out a toki — like an axe — but it was okay. People were just expressing their mamae and frustration. It was good to see everyone get their say and everything worked out in the end. The vote to put things in the hands of a few didn't go ahead.

There were a few other fractious hui when our iwi was debating the Central North Island Forests Deed of Settlement, eventually signed in 2008. The deal provided redress for iwi in the area over historical Te Tiriti o Waitangi breaches connected to land seized by the Crown for state forests — thousands and thousands of hectares. All those trees you see when you drive through the central North Island, those massive forests? Yeah, they were planted on Māori land taken by the Crown.

As well as the CNI deal, our iwi, Ngāti Rangitihi, also set about negotiating with the Crown to settle Treaty grievances specific to us. This is a complicated and drawn-out exercise, both internally and externally. There were about twelve years between the beginning of talks and the signing of a deal.

In each case, the deals meant an iwi that had been made poor for five or six generations came into some pūtea. Inevitably that meant a few bust-ups and fights as people scrapped over the funds. Some people were trying to cut other people's throats to get their hands on it. I get why the divisions happened: when people who've had nothing see something, they want a part of it. But I'm glad me and my cousins, especially Hori, got a reputation for going down and stopping any bullying that was going on.

Looking back, me being involved in the back and forth, going to the hui, standing up for things, and being exposed to the Treaty process would help me deal with things that were to happen in the years ahead. It would also give me an idea which I hope will change the country forever.

But that was all ahead of me.

+ + +

With Nana having passed, and unsure of what my future held, I went to stay with one of my aunties in Sandringham. It was the perfect place for me to spend time reconsidering what I wanted to do with my life.

So much had happened. Caring for Nana had reminded me of those years when she and Koro looked after me and nurtured me. Being taken off them when I was six had sent my life into a gruesome spiral of abuse and torture. At age fourteen I was both angry and dead inside, not giving a fuck about much and ready to cause havoc. In my twenties I'd fled to Australia where the turmoil continued, even as I tried to escape my past torment. I'd come home in my thirties, once again getting away as the pressure threatened to crush me.

My whole life I'd been moving on, knowing that things weren't right, that there was more to life, that I couldn't stay where I was: that voice in my head at Waikeria Prison; the thoughts that came to me in the junkie house in Sydney and made me jump on a train to Adelaide; the realisation at the bikie club that there was danger on the horizon, that I could stay and be a high-level gangster or I could walk away; and seeing the future out the plane window as I flew back to Aotearoa but not being able to define exactly what that future was.

It doesn't have to be this way. It doesn't have to be this way. It doesn't have to be this way.

But what way could it be? Where should I take my life? Could I find any meaning other than the escape routes I'd previously sought — petrol, glue, booze, drugs, gangs, money — which had all turned out to be dead ends?

Living at Aunty's house, figuring things out, I came to a firm decision: *I'm not going to do anything criminal anymore. I'm done.* One of the good things that had come out of my exposure to the Māori Party was that it put me on a new path, one of wanting to uplift my people. And I knew I couldn't do that as a criminal. *That* was never going to work. If I carried on with crime it would only ever benefit me, even if I'd once dreamed of being the socialist criminal who spread the money around like a modern-day Robin Hood.

By stepping away from that world, I could find a better way to help people — not that I knew what that looked like yet. But it felt like a momentous decision.

To progress, though, I was going to need to study. Even though I wasn't aware of it at the time, somewhere inside me the words and encouragement of Mary Kayes — the teacher who had taken me in and desperately tried to help me — must have come to the fore: education was the first step. But how was that going to happen for someone who'd effectively given up on school when they were barely a teenager? And what did I want to study? I needed to find something to get the momentum going.

+ + +

Not long afterwards, I was sitting on a bus headed for Greenlane. My destination? The New Zealand College of Chinese Medicine. I'd enrolled to study acupuncture and turned up for my first day, one of the few non-Asian people doing it. And I loved it.

Why acupuncture? Why not something like motor mechanics, or even horticulture, a field I'd shown a flare for? I actually don't know. Maybe those months spent in caring roles looking after my relatives, especially my uncle and my nana, gave me the idea of something in the realm of healthcare. And I certainly had some history with needles . . . albeit in a completely different context.

When they started teaching us how to insert the needles and what it was all about, I turned out to be a bit of a natural. My understanding of the concept and its holistic nature resonated. I don't know why, but I just *got* it. Acupuncture is a way of communicating with the body, of figuring out the underlying problems and telling the body how it can bring balance to itself. No medicine; just needles manipulating specific points in the body.

So when it came to the practical side, I was on point. But the books and study side? That was a struggle. I guess it came out of all those years of voices telling me I was shit; all those years of missing out on formal education. Reading was fine — I was good at reading, always had been. But exams and tests, I found hard. Even though my knowledge and understanding could be locked in — I could sit there and talk with someone about it like a pro — in an exam situation I'd run into problems. Things just wouldn't connect; I'd read a question wrong, or read too much into it, overcomplicate it, and end up thinking: *What the fuck is this saying?*

If there was one thing I'd learned over the years, though, it was that if I put my mind to something, you better bet I'm going to make it. You ain't gonna stop me. Single-mindedness is hard-wired into me. When I have a goal in mind, I'm going to achieve it — or die trying. That's the part of my psyche I turned to now. While I was never going to be top of the class, I would read and read and read and go over things a hundred times until they stuck in my head.

All those skills of determination, of survival, of sheer stubbornness and steadfastness — they proved their worth again. But where once those traits had been used to overcome hostility, profit from deals, see hidden risks and threats, now they were helping me learn anatomy and the core concepts of this ancient Asian practice.

I was learning more than just what was in the books, too; I was also learning good habits. Turning up to class on time, applying myself to achieve the standard I needed to gain the qualification, fitting into the system; albeit in a way that suited my style and without compromising who I was.

Acupuncture helped me find something else in those three

years — yes, it was a three-year course, not some night classes or something like that; this was serious stuff. It helped me discover what my future might be: a future of hope, and of progress. I had been looking for what I might do after I was finished studying. And I thought I'd found it.

As part of the practical learning required on the course, we used to go to marae to offer acupuncture clinics. For instance, we went to the Poukai — big celebrations where the Kīngi Māori goes to visit marae associated with the Kīngitanga movement. It's all about celebrating Kīngitanga and sustaining the marae. We'd follow the Poukai around and do acupuncture for anyone who'd come along. I loved it, and I started to think: *I could do this. Set myself up with a couple of massage tables, chuck the tables in the back of a station wagon and go around to marae helping kaumātua and kuia with their pains.* Helping the people, but also earning money.

Once I'd graduated, I gave it a go. It was awesome to feel part of a wider kaupapa, to feel the wairua and kotahitanga. But unfortunately there was no money in it and it wasn't sustainable. I'd thought I'd be able to earn some money through ACC, but they wouldn't cover acupuncture at the time unless you had a clinic, and so I was just working for koha. I was happy and content, but I needed to be sensible and I knew this wasn't going to last.

Acupuncture had set me on a positive path, helped me learn good habits and gave me confidence learning again. But I needed more. I guess you could say it was another *It doesn't have to be this way* moment. This one, though, was a lot gentler and more forgiving. It wasn't me rejecting something, or realising my ways needed to change; more an understanding that I'd come closer to finding my way but this wasn't quite it.

Once more, I needed to think what my way might be — and I found an answer I hadn't expected.

Chapter 14

Lights and Sirens

Despite learning so much in those three years of learning acupuncture, including good study and work habits, ultimately it hadn't led to a career. I wasn't crushed or disillusioned by that, though. Instead it got me thinking about what it was I *really* wanted to do.

There were things about acupuncture, and the idea I'd had about travelling around marae as a roving therapist, that started to guide me in a new direction. I loved being out in the community, having that engagement with people; I loved the challenge of figuring out what the person in front of me needed to help them get better, and then applying a solution; and I loved the autonomy.

Whatever I did next, then, I knew it needed to involve me being in the community, finding a solution to a challenge and being autonomous. So I did what everyone does these days: I jumped on the internet. I tapped in search after search, scrolling through result after result. *Nope, nope, nope* . . . and then, *Yep — that's it!*

As soon as I saw it I knew this was the direction I wanted to go in: I wanted to be a paramedic. Jumping on an ambulance, heading out to emergencies large and small, and serving people who needed help. The website said: 'Paramedics often work independently in remote or difficult environments and have to make critical, often complex decisions.' This was the career that would tick all three of my boxes.

I looked up how you could join, and the most obvious pathway for me in Auckland was via AUT, at their university campus on the North Shore. More study, but I wasn't daunted by that. I'd have to apply to study the paramedicine major in the Bachelor of Health Science degree, another three years with a mix of theory and practical experience. I read all the requirements to apply, and it was all good; except for one thing. Because of the practical part — going out in the community with ambulances — I'd need a police clearance.

By now, I hadn't been in trouble for about twenty years — almost. Not long after I'd come back to New Zealand, I had a car accident. Coming down the winding roads around Waiwera Hot Pools, north of Auckland, one day in 2005, my car hit an oil spot, spun out and landed in a ditch. I was sober and the police acknowledged that I was keeping to the speed limit. But I got charged with careless driving.

On the day I appeared in the North Shore District Court, everyone else on similar charges got diversion — which is where nothing goes on your criminal record so long as you admit what you've done. That wasn't offered to me as an option. But I decided to plead guilty anyway to get it over and done with. In front of the judge, the prosecutor was making a big song and dance about my case; but then said, quietly, that I had no previous convictions. The ones I'd had were all when I was a juvenile, so they couldn't be used against me now I'd been clean for so long.

The judge was clearly wondering what was going on, and a bit confused as to why I wasn't being offered diversion. Meanwhile, the prosecutor just stood there, saying nothing. I explained things to the judge: 'Things happened years ago when I was a juvenile. I haven't been in trouble since.'

'Ah,' said the judge. And he gave me a small fine and didn't even take my licence off me.

But now I'd been convicted again, my entire previous record could be accessed. I knew that when I applied for police clearance AUT would see everything. So I was upfront in my application. I said I'd had the recent driving charge, explaining what had happened, and that up until then I hadn't been in trouble for twenty years. 'I'm seeking to better my life through this new career,' I wrote.

I crossed my fingers, but in the back of my mind I knew what the outcome was going to be. And sure enough, I got knocked back. I was allowed to complete the theory papers, but I couldn't do the practical work on the ambulances, which started after six months of study.

It takes a lot to knock me off track, though. Single-mindedness, determination, stubbornness, overcoming adversity — yeah, that's me. So I kept studying more papers while I waited to re-apply. I guess I must have proved myself somehow, because the second time around I was accepted. I was away. There seemed to be a bit of tension, but I didn't care. I knew what I had to do: study hard and prove wrong anyone who doubted me.

Maybe those extra six months of studying the theory papers helped, because I was really on to it. I picked things up quickly, did all the extra tutorials, extra reading, and was even tutoring some of the other students. By the end of the second year, I had an A average and was in the top 3% of my class. I was the top mature Māori student at AUT. All I had to do was finish my final year, soak up that work experience on the ambulance shifts, and I'd be on track.

It made me feel proud to look back at how much things had changed for me, through discipline, hard work — and being given the opportunities I so often hadn't. I even had a little bit of money thanks to a part-time job I'd found in my first year.

There was no stopping me now.

+ + +

Halfway through my first year of paramedicine, I'd started working at the Salvation Army Bridge programme. It felt like a nice rounding-out of the circle since I'd had help myself from them when I started my recovery in Adelaide all those years ago. A little bit of giving back.

I'd had to get a police clearance again, and when it came back the manager called me in and said: 'Tim, we've had discussions after your clearance came back from the police, and we're not going to go with the advice they've given us — we're going to hire you.' It felt good that they believed in me despite what the police said about my past.

The job was two shifts a week, working midnight to 8 a.m. on Fridays and Saturdays, in Mt Eden, central Auckland. The Bridge programme provided residential drug and alcohol rehabilitation. At any one time there were about twelve to fourteen residents, both males and females, and my job was to make sure the place was safe for them during the night and to get them up in the morning for breakfast. New residents arrived on a Friday, so it was particularly important to make sure they felt comfortable and weren't freaking out in their new environment.

I really enjoyed the work — getting paid was good, of course, and so was the free food, although it didn't do anything for my weight — but it also felt good to be helping people out. I had a real affinity with the residents, and I got on well with lots of them. I was able to use my past experiences to offer them some solid support, and I could have decent chats with some of them, talking about their problems and challenges.

One morning, while going to each room to wake everyone up, I walked into the room of a new resident who I had known from the old days. We'd grown up on the street together. He'd just been released from Pāremoremo prison after an eleven-year sentence and was at Bridge as part of his release plan before he went back into the community. On the Saturday morning when

I woke him up, I said, 'Is that you, bro?' And he went, 'Hey, man, I haven't seen you for ages!' We talked and talked, reminiscing about the old times and people we both knew. There were a few guys we both knew who'd passed away, so we remembered them, too. It was a great kōrero.

After about twenty minutes, though, I realised we'd run out of things to say. Since the time we'd known each other as teenagers we'd gone different ways, taken different paths. When I faced a decision about doubling down and remaining a gangster I'd opted not to, and changed direction. We were now two different people.

It wasn't as simple as making personal choices, either. So many of the guys I'd grown up with were in the life he was because they'd been denied the opportunity to develop their potential — instead being pushed down and pushed out of society, marginalised and imprisoned. Imagine if they didn't have to overcome the shit that comes with being more likely to be arrested and prosecuted, more likely to leave school without qualifications, more likely to die young of diseases and other health conditions — not to mention having to deal with racism their whole lives. How many of them would have become teachers, scientists, lawyers, doctors? Some of them went on to have leadership positions in gangs — no disrespect, but what if they'd instead ended up in business, or running big mainstream organisations? With their brains and their skills, anything would be possible.

As I sat there with this guy I'd known from another life, I couldn't help but imagine all that happening. In the movie version of my life you could dramatise this by having a scene where I was looking to my past, glimpsing a life I'd left behind; a sliding doors moment. It wasn't like that at all. I was not looking at him and thinking, *That could have been me*, because I was very happy with where I was. And I was certainly not criticising his choices, or judging him in any way at all — that's not who I am. I just became very aware that I felt uncomfortable. Don't get me wrong; I've felt uncomfortable almost every day of my life, so it was no big deal. I was just acutely aware that we were different, and we'd run out of things to talk about.

So I just said, 'I'm going to go now.' And he went, 'Yeah, cool, cool.' And that was it.

+ + +

With the studying and the job, I felt my life was on track. I was getting a lot out of life, and putting a lot back in. I wasn't drinking, and I hadn't touched drugs since before I left Adelaide. Things were good, and on the up.

And then 29 July 2012 happened. An incident which tipped my life upside down and threw everything into disarray. The ground was about to shift beneath me, setting me on a collision course with chaos; destiny was hurling a cruel twist in my direction.

It started innocently enough. During handover when I arrived at the Bridge centre at midnight, I was told the police had brought one of the clients back from weekend leave because he was drunk. He was a diabetic, and the booze had reduced his sugar levels to the point where an ambulance had to be called. He'd stabilised once he got back to the centre, so my job was just to keep an eye on him, to monitor him regularly and make sure his blood sugar didn't lapse back into the danger zone.

An easy enough task for me, one I'd done many times before. But still, I needed to be diligent and focused. So that's exactly what I was doing. About 2.30 a.m., I had a meal in the TV room and then went to check on the guy. Everything was fine. But when I walked out of his room, I heard a man's voice yelling. I couldn't make out where it was coming from, as it was echoing through the corridors. It was loud, but I couldn't make out what he was saying; just the occasional 'Fuck this' and 'Fuck'. And it seemed like he was on the move.

My main concern was the safety of the residents. I went from one end of the building to the other, desperately trying to figure out what the fuck was going on. Then I heard glass breaking, but with the noise echoing everywhere it still wasn't clear where all this was happening, and who was doing it. *It must be outside*, I thought. I rushed to the office to grab a torch, then headed to the foyer. And sure enough: broken glass all over the floor — the front door had been smashed in. This was getting really worrying. Whoever this was, I needed to find them fast.

I stepped outside and walked down the side of the building, which backed on to a park right beside Dominion Road, one of Auckland's most famous roads. Standing in the park, shining my light around, I heard the same voice again, swearing away. *Fuck, that's him.* I spotted him out in the middle of the road — he was actually trying to kick a taxi. He was stumbling around, clearly drunk as. I decided to go talk to him and bring him back to the centre where I could keep him safe and call the police.

By the time I got to the road, he'd crossed over to the other side and was staggering along, still swearing and carrying on. He looked quite dishevelled and quite old, though he turned out to be only 47. I kept heading towards him. 'Bro, I know what you've done. We need to go back to the office,' I said to him. He said something back, but he was slurring so much all I could make out was the word 'fuck'. I said: 'Bro, please don't do this. Come on — let's just go back to the office.' I did not need this.

If only he'd listened to me. If only we'd gone back to the office. If only. If only.

Instead, he took a fast step towards me. I thought he was going to hit me, so I raised my hand up to push him away. He fell, and hit his head on the concrete. And he hit it hard. *Bang.*

Straight away, my instinct and training kicked in — *I've got to help this guy.* I could see a few drops of blood coming from his nose, and he was making snoring sounds. I knew that sound meant his airway was somehow compromised and that keeping him breathing was my top priority. So I knelt beside him, rolled him over on to his side to keep his airway open and to let the blood flow freely. With my left hand, I pulled my phone out of my pocket and rang 111 to call an ambulance. I felt for his carotid pulse, which was weak.

When I listened to that 111 call later, I could hear the urgency in my voice. 'Tell me exactly what happened,' the operator said. 'This guy is on the ground . . . he's bleeding from the mouth . . . I heard him yelling . . . I'm working at the drug rehab . . . he actually kicked in our door and I've chased him down the street.'

My thoughts were for his safety, but also: *I didn't do anything wrong.*

By that point, a car had stopped and someone called out to ask if I needed help. 'Yes, please,' I yelled. They got out of the car, and I handed the phone to them so I could keep on managing the guy's airway.

I was freaking out. *I didn't do anything wrong.*

He was still breathing, and I had the airway clear, so I was telling myself to just keep doing what I was doing and wait for the ambulance to get there.

Then, out of nowhere, a drunk guy came across the street. And it was like he'd found his prime opportunity to be the centre of attention. He started screaming at me. 'Why the fuck did you hit him?'

'Bro, I didn't hit him,' I said.

'You fucking did!' And he just kept on swearing at me.

I didn't have time to argue, so I just kept focusing on the unconscious guy, keeping him breathing. The drunk guy yelled: 'I'm ringing the police!' He was on the phone, screaming down the phone telling them he'd watched me assault the guy. It was utter bullshit, but what could I do? One of the people from the car told the guy to shut up. Everything went quiet. There was just the sound of the unconscious guy's heavy, slow breathing, like a loud snore. And then came the sirens.

The ambulance arrived, and I filled them in about the patient's condition. I was in shock — it was traumatic. At one point, one of the ambulance officers asked me if I'd hit him with my torch or my hand.

What? Were they implying something? *I didn't do anything wrong.* I pointed to my palm and said it was my hand.

As they loaded the man into the ambulance, the police said they wanted to talk to me. What could I do but go along with that? We went over to the Bridge office. An officer asked me to tell him what happened. I started talking — I had nothing to hide. Then his phone rang; he listened to what was being said, and hung up with a grave look on his face.

'Tim, I'm going to have to stop this interview now. The patient has gone status one, so we're gonna have to wait for the detectives to get here.' Status one is a medical term for someone who is critical; in other words, they're in danger of dying.

My head was spinning. But I knew exactly what was going on: I felt like I was being set up to see if I would say something incriminating. The situation was being ramped up, with talk of status one and detectives . . . putting on the pressure.

I didn't do anything wrong.

When the detectives arrived, they took me to the Auckland Central station. As they led me to the car, I tried to stay calm and kept on being cooperative. Sitting in the back, looking out the window, watching the car headlights and lights in the shops along Dominion Road blur past, I dreaded to think where this journey would take me. Of course, it was not my first time going through something like this. But this time the stakes were extremely high.

I was placed in an interview room with a camera. It was about six in the morning by that stage, and I was exhausted and stressed. I put my head down on the desk. But there was no time for sleep. They pressed on with the interview. Again, I had to go through what happened. But it was all a blur, and I couldn't remember what I'd said. Later, I'd learn there was something I did during that interview that the police would try to use against me.

Once the interview was done, they took my clothes off me, put me in a white boiler-suit, photographed me, and took a DNA swab from my mouth.

I'd come so far in my life, and yet here I was again. Except this time I hoped it would be over soon. It was so obvious that I had pushed him away in self-defence, but because he was so drunk he had fallen badly. That was it. An awful situation. *But I didn't do anything wrong.*

The man lay in a coma in hospital while a police investigation began. About a week later, I got told he had died. It was now a homicide investigation, and there was only one person the police were interested in: me.

Chapter 15

The Trial

Head down, rain smacking straight into me . . . but on I'd march. Forward, forward, forward. All I could do was get up every day and keep going — whatever was in front of me, whatever the weather, whatever noises my hungry stomach made. I had hardly any money; just sheer determination. In my view, I had no choice but to keep going. Stopping or going backwards was a pathway to destruction.

It went like this for month after month. Each day, my alarm would go off first thing; I'd get up and walk from Mt Eden into the central city, rain, hail or shine; hop on an AUT shuttle bus to the North Shore campus; sit in the classroom, trying my best to focus on my studies; get on the shuttle bus to return to the city; walk home to my hostel; eat a meagre meal in my room; go to sleep.

The next day it would be the same. Day after day. *Forward, forward, forward. Don't stop. Don't look back.*

This very simple routine was what I needed to stay alive; it was all I had. This very simple routine just needed to be done. Because *fuck them*. Because I hadn't done anything wrong. *I hadn't done anything wrong.*

My life was in a tailspin that had started the night I went outside to see what all the noise and broken glass was about and saw a man crossing Dominion Road — and once again became the centre of an unwavering police investigation.

\+ + +

Let's rewind a few months. As the sun came up the morning after the incident, when the police were done interviewing me on video, photographing me, taking a DNA sample, they arranged for a cop to drop me home.

I knew this wasn't purely altruistic. They were checking me out. And I knew they would keep doing so from now on. I was under intense scrutiny; they were going to search for anything they could to prove a case against me.

The cop dropping me home said, 'I'll walk you to the door.' I knew the drill, so I said, 'Okay, cool.' I knew he wanted to take a 'casual' look in my room, to see if there was anything they could use as evidence to demonstrate I was a bad guy. Of course I knew there was nothing, so I said, 'Come on in.'

There were no beer bottles, no bongs, nothing — because I was clean as.

He walked around the place. 'Oh, it's quite nice, eh?'

'Yeah, mate, it is.'

'Okay, I'll see you later.'

'Yep, thanks for the lift.'

And then I was on my own. And it hit me. *What the fuck?!* Once again, I felt like I had a target on my back. Once again, I was in the glare, the spotlight of police who would no doubt have already looked up my history and fixated on that rather than all the good I was doing with my life now.

I plunged into a depressive state once more. But I knew I had to keep going. *Forward, forward, forward.*

On Monday I turned up to university and told them what had happened. Initially, everyone acted normally. But then later in the week, people's behaviour towards me changed. I guessed the cops had been to see them. They were cranking up their investigation after the guy died, eight days after he'd hit his head on the road. I was the only 'person of interest' in a homicide inquiry.

And it wasn't just the cops who were interested in what had happened. All sorts of people started asking me very specific questions about what I'd done. Like, I was offered counselling by the Bridge programme. A psychiatrist came around to see me. Of course I needed help — I was depressed. But I was on my guard. And sure enough, after the psychiatrist sat down with me he said: 'Tim, I need to tell you that anything you tell me may be passed on to the police.'

There was nothing to tell — I'd only ever told the truth about what happened: that the guy was really drunk, he'd smashed the windows, and when I went to speak to him about it, he stepped in towards me. I thought he was attacking me and I pushed him away; he fell to the ground and hit his head. It was tragic, it was awful. But I'd done nothing wrong.

The psychiatrist started digging in with probing questions, as if he was fishing for some kind of confession. It was like he was trying to trick me into saying I wanted to hit this guy, or I'd somehow provoked a situation. I knew that wasn't true. So all I said was: 'I let him get too close to me.'

He said: 'Oh, could that have made him want to do something?'

What's he getting at? I didn't know, so I just said: 'I don't know. We got too close and because he moved forward, I just had a natural reaction.' There were more questions like that, none of which seemed to be about my wellbeing, which was what I had thought the session was for.

Eventually, he looked at his watch. I think he realised he wasn't getting anywhere — because there was nowhere to get. He left, and I never heard from him again. The whole thing was a waste of time, which was unfortunate; I could really have used some help.

+ + +

During that period, I was also coping with some other very heavy emotions. My mum had been diagnosed with lung cancer and was rapidly deteriorating. But because of everything that was going on with the case, and her illness being so sudden, I never got to do things I should have been doing with her: making one last effort to get some closure, or at least talk about how it had been for me growing up. There was just no time, plus I was so messed up with worry about whether I was going to be charged. We only had about four weeks between the diagnosis and her passing away.

About a year after Mum passed away, my stepfather got sick and died, too. It's hard to explain, but I just felt nothing, no emotion. It was different with Mum: after she was gone, guilt and anguish festered inside me — and would stay there for years; all because instead of being able to grieve for my mum, I was consumed with the thought of being sent to prison for something I didn't do.

While the case was ongoing, I also lost someone else who was precious to me. Mary Kayes — the woman who believed in me even if I didn't, the woman who tried and tried to give me a home — had a stroke. I went and visited her, and we had lunch. She was ecstatic that I was studying. Because I didn't want to upset her, I didn't say a word about the case. Mary passed away soon after I saw her. And once again, I never got the chance to grieve, to mourn for this woman who had done so much for me.

Because by then, things had become very serious.

+ + +

Less than a week after I'd buried my mum, about seven weeks after the incident, the police called and asked me to come into the station. 'We just want to go over a few details, fill out a few parts,' the cop said to me.

Something told me it was time to get a lawyer, so I rang a pastor who I used to do acupuncture for and asked him if he knew one. He said he'd sort one but, in the meantime, I shouldn't talk to anyone. 'Just tell them you've got a lawyer on the way, and you don't want to speak.'

At the station, I met the cop who'd called me. He took me to a room where he'd already set up a screen showing the video interview I'd done on the first night, and played the whole thing back to me.

There was one moment in particular I noticed. And immediately I knew it was the moment the police were zeroing in on. I watched it closely. I watched the cop closely. I could see this was the thing they were going to try to hang a case against me on. However, despite what they'd seen, or thought they'd seen, I still knew I hadn't done anything wrong.

After the video finished playing, the detective said he had a few questions. But I stopped him.

'I think I need a lawyer, and I've got one coming,' I said.

'Oh, it's okay, we've got one here you can talk to,' he replied. They had a lawyer on speed dial ready for me.

'Nah, I'll wait for my one,' I said.

He looked pissed off, but there wasn't anything he could do. 'Look, Tim, we know you've not been getting into any trouble, you're not doing anything.' They really had been digging around. And of course they'd come up with nothing. I'd walked through some shit, but I was now on the other side. My life was a different life now. Except now I had a sense of dread deep in my stomach.

+ + +

My lawyer came with me to the police station the next day. Initially, I felt confident things would work out; that I'd have someone to help me prove my innocence. Then she went off into a room with the police by herself, and they talked without me there. I was thinking: *What the fuck's this all about?*

When she came back, she said to me: 'Tim, they're going to charge you, but they're going to give you bail.' That meant I wasn't going to prison to wait for the case to be heard. At least that was something.

I kept waiting for her to tell me what they'd been talking about, but she said nothing. It was so strange. I don't know what the cops had told her but I felt like I was on my own from that moment on.

I was charged with manslaughter, meaning the police were alleging his death was the consequence of me hitting him, even if I hadn't intended killing him. The cops were accusing me of killing a man I'd gone to ask why he was breaking the windows at the Bridge programme, a man I'd rolled on to his side to clear his airways, a man I'd called an ambulance for. I couldn't make sense of it. I hadn't done anything wrong.

Even though I was depressed, I had to just put my head down and get on with things. Then I got splashed across the pages of the *Herald on Sunday* newspaper. 'Worker on death charge,' read the headline. 'Wannabe politician charged after a clash at Salvation Army centre.'

They used my name, said I was studying to be a paramedic, and brought up my previous connections with the Māori Party. (I'd been way down on the list during the previous election, 2011, with virtually no hope of getting in, but hadn't had much to do with the party since then, concentrating instead on my studies.) It was utter clickbait. But it now meant I was going to struggle to keep my head down.

In the meantime, the Salvation Army told me I couldn't work at the Bridge while there was a court case. Fair enough, but no work meant no pay. Uni had also told me I wasn't going to be able to carry on with my ambulance shifts, the practical part of my studies. Without those, I wasn't going to be able to graduate. I could keep studying theory papers, but because I was no longer considered a full-time student I was no longer entitled to any allowances.

I was broke. And I was broken.

+ + +

This was what made me turn to the routine of just trying to keep going, both for my mental health and out of necessity. I had barely enough money for rent and a bit of food; no money for transport, let alone anything else. And so, I settled into my pattern: walking into town, getting the shuttle, sitting in the classroom, getting the shuttle back, walking home, eating what little I could afford to, going to bed, getting up the next morning to do it all over again. I did it without thinking about it, the routine as instinctive and mindless as breathing and just as important in keeping me going.

I buckled down to my studies, even though my grades suffered, sliding from an A-minus to a C-minus.

But there was no way I was letting anyone beat me now. I knew how far I'd come, what I had endured, what I had persevered through, what I had overcome. I needed to weather this storm, too, and carry on with the single-mindedness that had worked for me in the past. Besides, getting through this was the only way I could provide a future for my son.

He was the reason I *had* to carry on.

Everyone else expected me to give up. The easy thing to do was quit fighting, quit my studies, and just let the system dictate how things would turn out, to take what was coming to me. *Well, fuck that*, I thought. *I'm gonna get my day in court, and I'm going to prove you all wrong.*

As the court hearing got closer, I knew that the only person I could rely on if I was to walk free was me. At one point, my lawyer came to me after talking to the prosecution without me being present again. She told me they had a deal for me. 'Tim, they've got a strong case and they say if you plead guilty you'll get three-and-a-half years,' she said.

'Oh, really,' I said.

'Yeah, they've got a strong case, a really strong case,' she repeated.

In my head I thought: *What the fuck? Have you even seen the evidence?* But I kept calm and just said: 'I'm sorry, I'm not taking the deal.' It was a risk, because if I was found guilty I'd probably get a longer sentence. But there was no way I was confessing to manslaughter, with the maximum sentence of life imprisonment.

In the build-up to the trial, things became even more tense with my lawyer. She'd shown me something called the disclosure file — a copy of all the documents being relied on by the prosecution. In there was a document which allegedly laid out my criminal record, but it was a shambles. For instance, it showed a conviction for being an unlicensed driver in 2007. That was wrong. It never happened. What was going on?

The more I went through things, the more obvious it was that this whole document was an absolute disgrace. Nothing apart from my address and date of birth was correct. They'd spelt my name wrong, the photo was of another Māori man and the prior convictions listed included some for violent crimes I knew nothing about. The whole thing was a massive mistake. Right at the time I'd been falsely accused of killing someone, it heightened my sense that the police had it in for me.

I wanted everything corrected immediately. But when I emailed my lawyer about it, she brushed it off and told me to go into the court to sort it out myself. 'I cannot do this for you as I am assigned only to the manslaughter charge,' she wrote.

It didn't seem right to me. If it was in the disclosure file, surely it was part of the manslaughter case? And what about justice? It seemed like yet another example of how I was on my own against the system.

\+ + +

Finally, twelve months after I was charged, the trial began, in the High Court at Auckland. My whānau, including my cousins, were there for me. They believed in me, even if no one else did. Yet the case against me seemed so thin. There were more than 30 prosecution witnesses, but as they gave evidence they seemed more like defence witnesses, backing up what *I'd* said.

The people from the car which pulled up after the guy fell to the ground confirmed that I was caring for him and was on the phone to the ambulance. One of my bosses from the Salvation Army said I was excellent, and talked about a previous incident which I'd handled well. Other witnesses talked about the guy who'd died, saying that he suffered from alcohol addiction, and described incidents where he would lose his temper and get aggressive when he was drunk.

There was evidence he had been drinking heavily for many hours before our encounter. It even turned out there had been a very similar incident the same night. He'd gone into a liquor store trying to buy some bourbon and cola, but since he was already heavily intoxicated they wouldn't serve him. He was told to leave the store, which he didn't take well. Making a fist with his right hand, he raised it and took a swing but missed. 'I could stab you in the eye with a pen,' he told staff. He got pushed out of the store and ended up tripping over on to his back on the pavement. It was spookily like what had happened with me, except in my case the guy hit his head on the concrete. And everything at the liquor store was captured on CCTV cameras, so the jury got to see the incident for themselves.

The main witness against me was the dickhead who had run across the road and started abusing me while we were trying to care for the guy on the ground. When the people from the car who'd stopped gave evidence, they confirmed that this guy, who had also been drinking, was being a pain and not helping the situation. But none of that was relevant. What was important to the police case was that this guy claimed to have been an eyewitness to the crucial seconds of the encounter between me and the guy who died. The only eyewitness. This was critical.

Then he was asked if he'd seen me hit the guy.

'Oh, no,' he said. The guy hadn't even seen me hit him, and he was the Crown's main witness? I couldn't believe it.

When it was time for the pathologist to give evidence, he was asked his opinion about a cut on the guy's lip. Could it have been caused by a punch? The pathologist said, yes, it could have been. This was what the Crown case was coming down to: had I used a punch or a palm? Ever since my first interview, I'd said I had used my palm. Which was true. But the Crown was trying to show it was a punch.

The judge asked the pathologist if the cut on the guy's lip could have been from a palm rather than a punch. The pathologist said he didn't think so because of the amount of force that would have been needed to split the skin. That did seem weird to me; if you go on YouTube you can see guys breaking blocks of wood and things with their palms. But anyway . . .

The judge followed up, asking what if the victim was drunk? Well, yes, said the pathologist, that would change things. But, said the pathologist, he didn't know the guy was drunk because no toxicology tests were done. It was crazy. *Everyone* who goes to hospital when there's a police investigation under way gets screened for alcohol — why wasn't this guy?

From that point on, the scales seemed to be tipping in my favour. But it wasn't over yet.

It was my turn to take the stand, to answer questions from the prosecution. The answers I gave could determine my future; could help decide if I was going to be free to go back to my studies — or was going back to jail. As I walked up towards the witness box, I sensed it was going to come down to one moment, that moment I'd seen in the video when I'd been shown it in the police station.

During that interview, in the early hours of the morning soon after the incident, I'd been asked to talk the police through what happened, and to show them what I'd done. And in that moment, I'd demonstrated my actions with a closed fist. A punch, not a palm. This was what it was all coming down to.

Chapter 16

Guilty or Not Guilty?

During the trial, and leading up to it, I remember times when I'd think, *Yeah, this is not good. I'm going back inside.* In my head, I was preparing myself to go back to prison. Although I knew I hadn't done anything wrong, everything seemed stacked against me.

I'd tried so hard to change my life, to contribute to society, but it felt like everything had been wiped out in an instant. All that the police and prosecution perceived was an angry Māori guy who knew the inside of prison walls so well; who felt comfortable there. They wanted to send me back there, to the place I'd stepped out of two decades earlier.

I could feel all that pressure, all that scrutiny, all that judgement, bearing down on me.

I'd decided to give evidence in my own defence, knowing that this was my last chance to prove that I hadn't done anything wrong. In our system of justice, you're innocent until proven guilty. And I was innocent. But when you're the person in the middle? It doesn't feel like that. Things had been stacked against me, and it was going to come down to what I had to say.

The biggest threat to my freedom was on the video tape. When the guy stepped towards me and I thought he was going to hit me, I'd used the palm of my hand to fend him off; I'd contacted his face, and he'd fallen to the ground, probably not helped by just how much he'd had to drink. In every interview, every time I'd been asked, I'd said it was my palm.

Well, every interview but one . . . the video interview where I'd demonstrated what I'd done by closing my hand and forming a fist. It seemed to contradict what I'd been saying, and that was what the police had seized upon. They were insisting that I'd punched the guy. And the witness for that accusation — that was me, in that video.

I don't know why I did that, closed my fist. Straight after the incident, when I was first interviewed by the police near the scene, a cop recorded in his notebook that I'd said I hit him 'with an open hand'. And I'd said it to others too. But when I pulled my hand up on video, I had a closed fist. I can't explain it. But I knew I was about to be grilled about it.

When the prosecutor stood to start asking his questions, I sensed he thought I was just an idiot, some dumb fool he was going to take to task. Though it wouldn't have mattered if I *had* been dumb, because all I was going to do was tell the truth; say what happened.

He asked me to say what had happened, and I said to him that it was just like I'd said all along — pointing to the screen where the video of my interview had been played during the trial. This was the moment the prosecution was no doubt waiting for. The lawyer for the Crown zoned in, asking why the jury should believe I'd used my palm rather than my fist, especially given what I'd demonstrated in the video.

I replied: 'Because it's my understanding about the law.'

Smirking, he asked what I meant. I guess he figured I was going to say, 'Because I'm innocent until proven guilty and it's up to you to prove the case', or something like that.

Instead, I explained: 'When someone feels threatened, they can use force to defend themselves. And it doesn't matter whether the hand is open or closed — what matters is that the force is reasonable.'

In other words, the crucial point wasn't whether I'd used a palm or a fist — what mattered was that the force was a *reasonable* response to the situation. I'd said I'd used my palm because that was the truth. I had faith that things would work out if I just told the truth and didn't let myself get caught up in bullshit trying to argue about points that didn't matter. I didn't have to lie, anyway — I hadn't done anything wrong.

After I finished giving evidence, I stepped out of the witness box knowing I'd done everything I could — but also knowing that the outcome was not up to me. My future was going to come down to a decision from the twelve members of the jury.

When all the final formalities were out of the way, the jury was sent away to consider its verdict and I was led downstairs to the holding cells. I can't really describe how it felt to have your fate in other people's hands like that, knowing it would come down to what they believed.

At one point, the jury had a question about what 'reasonable' meant in the context of the trial. We all came back into court, and the judge scratched his head and just repeated what he'd said in his summing up. I was left scratching my head, too: what did their question mean?

Because I couldn't do anything more, because I couldn't influence what the jury was going to decide, I began preparing for the worst; preparing myself to go to prison. You can't go to prison with any emotion. I'd learned that lesson on my very first trip to Mt Eden, as a sixteen-year-old kid in the back of the van watching the older guys.

I started walking. Up and down the cell, side to side, around and around. I tried to walk out all my emotions, letting them trail behind me and fall to the cold ground with each step. Trampling over the discarded remains of my hope, my fear, my sadness and grief, my happiness. I stared at the ground as I walked, squelching everything out of me until there was nothing left but a shell. A shell ready to deal with whatever came next.

Finally, the call came to go back upstairs — there was a decision from the jury. I was numb, empty of emotion, as I stood up to hear their decision; whether I was guilty of manslaughter or not. I was so devoid of feeling that I almost didn't care what they said.

The foreman stood, and announced: 'Not guilty.'

They believed me. Not. Guilty. They understood I'd done nothing wrong. And yet all I could muster, in an almost monotonic response, was 'Oh, cool.' I thanked the jury, I thanked the judge, and I didn't even really see what the prosecution's reaction was.

At the back of the court, I hugged my cousins. They'd stood by me, believed me and supported me. I was so grateful. Apart from that, though, it was hard to know what to think. I suppose there was relief, but there certainly wasn't anything to celebrate — I had just been put through a massive ordeal for nothing.

\+ + +

Sometimes I think about an alternative universe, imagining a world in which things were different, where I wouldn't have been judged for my past. Where assumptions wouldn't have been made about me. A universe in which Māori and Pasifika don't have to deal with the worst of the justice system — the presumptions, the racial profiling, the prosecutions, the pressure to just plead guilty — more often than anyone else has to.

A universe in which I hear glass breaking while I'm at my workplace, a place where I have a duty to protect a group of vulnerable people. A universe where I go outside, stepping into a potentially dangerous situation and putting myself at risk, and find it's been caused by a guy who is absolutely obliterated drunk, unsteady on his feet, so I tell him we need to go back to the office to sort out what's happened — but also because it's no good having him wander the streets in the state he's in.

In this alternative universe, of course I'd prefer that what happened didn't happen, but let's just roll with it: he steps forward, I put up my hand to defend myself from him and it touches the side of the head. He doesn't have much balance, so he falls to the ground, he hits his head and slips into unconsciousness. I help him by putting him on his side, clearing his airways and ringing an ambulance straight away.

What happens next, in this alternative universe, is where things veer off in another direction. Instead of being charged with manslaughter, I'm thanked by my bosses for doing a good job, thanked for calling an ambulance, thanked for knowing what to do with this unconscious man. In this world, I'm asked if I'm okay, having gone through this traumatic experience. I'm not stopped from working, not stopped from graduating. My life and my dreams of making a difference are not put on hold.

+ + +

In the real world, in the aftermath of the trial I was left picking up the pieces. There were things I found out afterwards that compounded my sense that this wasn't right.

I found out that the police decided to charge me without first asking the Crown prosecutors to review whether they had enough evidence. They just went ahead with it. It also turned out that there had been a decision to not have a pre-trial hearing, where a judge would have had an opportunity to review the evidence. Surely the case would have been thrown out at this stage? I was told this was for cost-saving reasons; but seriously, what price is justice?

Then I realised the police could have dropped the case at any time: once they understood their witnesses were so weak; or as soon as they saw the video of the incident at the liquor store earlier that evening, showing the man acting exactly as I'd described him acting towards me. And yet the case kept going, dragging me through a living nightmare. All the evidence pointed to it being a very unfortunate accident caused by alcohol addiction and a day of heavy drinking. Instead, the whole thing was construed as being down to the uncontrolled violent temper of a Māori man.

All these things kept swirling around in my head as I went back to uni and tried to get back to earlier routines like going to the gym. But it was like I was carrying a heavy weight I couldn't let go of, the burden of the sense of injustice and the never-ending feeling of being under suspicion.

One day, in the car park at the gym, I couldn't get out of my car. I sat there thinking: *Fuck man, it doesn't matter how far I go in this life, it doesn't matter what I do, how much I achieve in this life, they're just waiting for any fucking thing to throw me off again. And they've got in their head that it doesn't matter what it is: 'When we get an opportunity we're going to fucking charge him and we're going to put him in prison. He deserves to be in prison, we don't want him out here, we want him in there.'*

I began thinking about how I could stop it; how I could shake those feelings loose. And then I had another realisation: *This isn't just happening to me; it's happening to all Māori. We're more than half of the prison population — which is way out of proportion. How many of them have a story like mine? Fucking heaps!*

There and then, in that car park, I decided I was going to do something to change that. Because if it wasn't going to be me, then who?

The first thing I did was complain to the Independent Police Conduct Authority, which reviews police actions. I was sure my case was clear-cut, that they'd come back and say that I shouldn't have been charged. It was a slam dunk. But no. The IPCA said the police hadn't done anything wrong.

I appealed; they reviewed it — same response. My only option was going to the High Court for a judicial review, but I had no money and, besides, what was the point? Everything seemed stacked against me. Again.

So that's when I thought: *You're Māori, mate. And you want to enhance things for all Māori. Let's take it to the Waitangi Tribunal.*

So that's what I did. I made an application to the Waitangi Tribunal, writing down everything that had happened during my case and how it had contravened Te Tiriti. I got back a reply that they'd received it, and it was given a number. And then I waited, and I waited.

In the meantime, I figured I needed some decent legal representation. I looked at other claims, and I came across one that had been made against Corrections. The claimant, a retired Corrections employee and a kaumātua, pointed out how the Crown had failed to reduce Māori reoffending rates and uphold policies specifically designed to help Māori inmates. The Tribunal found the Crown to be in breach of Te Tiriti and made a series of recommendations to fix things. It was a big deal. So I looked up who the lawyer was, and thought: *Yep, she'd be awesome!*

Her name was Roimata Smail. I got in touch, even though, to be honest, it wasn't a very appealing pitch I made to her. 'I'm just this guy trying to put in this claim, which is huge, but I've got no money, no prospects, no nothing,' I said. In return, she was going to have to put in a heap of time and effort. I guess it was no surprise that Roimata got back to me and said: 'Sorry, I'm really, really busy . . .' But maybe you've noticed that I don't give up easily. So I just kind of kept pestering her, and waiting until she wasn't so busy, or perhaps she just felt like I wasn't going to go away. Eventually, she took on the case. *Boom!*

Roimata worked on my statement of claim, and it was awesome, all lawyer-like. We resubmitted it, but still didn't hear anything back from the Tribunal for ages. But that was okay; I wasn't planning on going anywhere soon. I felt like I was on a crusade, that I knew what I wanted to happen and how I wanted to go about it. I was committed to making a difference for all Māori — now and into the future.

The claim itself called for an inquiry into the prosecution of Māori, pointing out the Crown's failure to address the disproportionate prosecution of Māori. It pointed out that Māori were charged and prosecuted in situations where non-Māori were not, and that — regardless of the outcome — there were consequences: irreversible damage and prejudice.

Sound familiar? Yeah, it was what I'd gone through with the manslaughter case.

The claim included my personal experiences, too. Not just with the manslaughter case; I went all the way back to when I was a kid getting in trouble all the time. I wrote: 'I'm not saying that I didn't do any of these things; like I said, I was a little shit. But the police were so all over me, and half the time the judge would see me and throw me in remand because they reckoned I was a menace who needed to be taken off the street to make it safe. Apart from a conviction for fighting in public, my only conviction for violence was throwing a Molotov cocktail in front of a bus.'

But my Tribunal claim wasn't just about me. It drew on evidence impacting all Māori, showing how Māori were prosecuted at a higher rate than non-Māori, leading to negative stereotypes about us being inherently criminal. It drew on evidence that police made decisions every day about whether to search, arrest and charge people — and Māori were always over-represented there. The claim pointed out that the Crown and the police had been aware of bias against Māori for years — a Police Commissioner even once admitted that there was 'unconscious bias' — but nothing had been done about it.

It was time for the Tribunal to intervene. That was the best place for it; I wanted it to be heard in public. And so I waited.

In the meantime, I got on with my life and my dream of becoming a paramedic. I'd been delayed, I'd been shaken, I'd been tested, but I was still determined. Even more than ever.

Chapter 17

The Meaning of Life

Now the manslaughter case was out of the way, I felt like I had my freedom back and I was determined to get started as a paramedic. I also got approached about featuring on a couple of TV programmes.

One was a current affairs programme called *Native Affairs*, on Māori Television (now Whakaata Māori). I did an interview about my case, and they also discussed it with a panel of politicians. One of them was the leader of the Māori Party at the time, Te Ururoa Flavell, and afterwards he apologised to me that the party hadn't helped out or offered much in the way of support during the court case. I appreciated him doing that.

Another of the politicians was New Zealand First leader Winston Peters. Now, I don't often agree with Peters, but he actually made an excellent point during the discussion. They were talking about the fact that I'd been left with a legal aid bill of $7440, which was due to start incurring interest of 8% per annum. Legal aid is money the government provides to help pay for your defence when you're charged with a crime. But it's not a handout — you have to pay it back.

It pissed me off that I was still lumbered with this debt even though I'd been charged for a crime I didn't commit and I'd been found not guilty. I decided there was no way I was going to pay it back — to do so would be like accepting that the system had the ability to punish me financially for a wrongful accusation. Kind of like, *We're going to abuse you and we're going to charge you for that abuse*. Fuck that.

On the programme, Peters said the police should have to pay for it. I couldn't believe it but he was absolutely right — if someone does something wrong, they get fined; they have to pay for their mistake. It's an incentive to not do certain things, right? So why shouldn't that apply to the police as well? I hadn't thought of it like that until Peters raised it — but it stuck in my head and I later added it to my submission to the Waitangi Tribunal. So I guess I have him to thank for the idea.

The other programme I was on was a documentary series called *I am Innocent*. It ran for a couple of seasons, featuring the stories of people who had been wrongly convicted or falsely accused. It was a mix of interviews, scenes where they would film me going about my daily life, and dramatisations. Some of it seemed a bit over the top, like when we were filming at the gym one of the film crew wanted me to put some boxing gloves on and do some sparring on camera. But I wasn't into that anymore, and it just seemed to be a bit of showboating. I said no. 'This is my story, I don't come to the gym and box, so it's not happening, okay?'

There was also a scene where they made me look like an informer. As I've said, my code is that I will not talk about the gangs I was with. That is their story to tell — I'm telling *my* story. And I stick to my code. But in talking to the producer, I slipped up and mentioned a couple of names of people who were in the club at the time. Those names ended up going in; and what was worse, it was put into the part of the story when I was talking about leaving the gang — though those people were not involved with that.

I pulled him up on it, telling him: 'What you've done is actually made me out to be an informer, and because you've put them into a part of the story they weren't involved with, you've also made me look like a liar. You've made shit up!' This experience has made me very wary about telling my story, and who I tell my story to.

+ + +

Once I'd completed my hours on the ambulance as a student and finally graduated, I couldn't wait to begin work. Once I started, however, I soon found out that while I loved the job I hated the company and the comments I would get. There were a lot of connections between the ambulance staff and police, not only through work but also through relationships and marriages between ambulance officers and cops.

I guess it should not have been a surprise that from the get-go, I encountered animosity and straight-out character assassination about the manslaughter case. In my first week I was on the ambulance with a senior officer and we dropped a patient off at Middlemore Hospital. As we were getting ready to leave again, she was talking to another paramedic. And when she jumped back in the cab, she turned to me and said: 'I was just talking to that guy about you, and he said you're a fucking killer and you shouldn't be here.'

I replied: 'You know I was found not guilty, and I didn't do anything, right?'

And she said: 'Yeah, but that's the feeling around here — you're a killer and you shouldn't be here.'

What was I supposed to say to that?

For a while, it was relentless. It was brought up constantly and I felt like I was under a lot of pressure. And because of that, I made silly mistakes. And those things built up against me, creating more pressure. I shut down and wouldn't talk to my partners in the ambulances, because I just didn't want to be having that conversation.

But that just compounded things. On one job, there was an old guy who was really sick and was also at the end of his life. Normally he'd have gone to hospital, but I asked him what he wanted to do. He knew the end was close, so he said: 'I just want to stay here.' I agreed to his request and we left. A few hours later, we got called again, and sure enough he'd died. A couple of weeks later I was partnered with an officer who was married to a cop. Out of the blue she brought up the case of the old man, and started asking me all these intense questions about it, making out like I was somehow responsible for his death.

I felt under constant scrutiny. The only thing that was keeping me there was the work — I loved it.

One day I got to experience the meaning of life all in one shift. There was a 'code red' call-out to Māngere; when you see an ambulance with its lights and sirens going, it means it's either a purple (a cardiac arrest) or a red (get there quick because it could turn into a purple). We pulled up to the house, headed inside and there was a woman in labour. When I say she was in labour — she was in the final stages of labour. The baby was on its way; there was no time to get her to hospital. So I delivered the baby right there, cut the umbilical cord, put him on her breast and delivered the placenta. The baby was healthy as: ten fingers, ten toes and screaming like fuck. We shot them off to hospital for a check-up. Beautiful job.

After that we soon got another call-out. It was a busy day, and we were heading all over the place, this way and that. Later in the shift, a call came in for a job in Henderson, out west, at a retirement village. Once we got there, I grabbed the paperwork from the office and my partner and I headed for this woman's room. As we rode up the elevator, I read what we were dealing with: an 89-year-old who had a lot of medical issues, including coronary heart disease, and who'd recently had a heart attack.

I got to the last page and there was a signed DNR — a Do Not Resuscitate form. She'd made up her mind that if her heart stopped, she didn't want us to do anything to revive her; she was ready to go. I told my partner so that we were on the same page: 'Bro, we're sick and we're DNR'd.' He said: 'Cool.'

We walked in, and she was in a bad way, lying on her back and doing what we call 'goldfishing': staring up with her mouth opening and closing. The main muscle responsible for breathing is our diaphragm. What it does is it flattens out, and when that happens the area in our lungs increases. That drops the pressure in our lungs and the air rushes in to equalise it — that's the mechanics of breathing. When someone is goldfishing, they're too weak for their diaphragm to pull down but their body knows it needs air so their mouth is opening and closing as if they're breathing, even though they're not. It's called agonal breathing.

We started giving her some oxygen so we could get her breathing under control. But I also knew she was in discomfort, even though she couldn't tell us anything. When you're in discomfort or pain, your heart rate increases and your blood pressure goes up. We could measure those things and see what was happening. So we gave her some morphine, monitoring her vital signs so we could see when she was less uncomfortable. We got the heart rate as close to 70 as we could, and the blood pressure as close to 100 as we could. All the while, she didn't have to tell us anything. We knew she was in a good place.

The centre had called her family, so I sat down beside her, and said: 'Love, your family will be here soon, the staff have called them and they're on their way now.' She gave the faintest of smiles, and then she passed away. She was ready to go, she wasn't in any pain, and she was happy, thinking of her family as she passed.

In one day, I'd helped someone come into the world and helped someone else leave it, and it was a privilege to be part of both: a good birth and a good death. It was the best day I ever had on the road.

\+ + +

There were also lots of crazy jobs — when you're in an ambulance racing to a call, you never quite know where you're going to end up. One call-out I'll never forget could easily start with the line: 'It was a dark and stormy night . . .'

The job was in Auckland, in an area I knew like the back of my hand. But as we turned into the street, with rain pelting down on the windscreen and the darkness enveloping us, it seemed utterly unfamiliar. It was like I'd driven to another dimension, another world — the scene of a horror movie.

Remember the classic movie *Psycho*? Or maybe you know the Netflix TV series based on it called *Bates Motel*, in which Norman Bates is a mild-mannered motelier who turns into a murderous psychopath. In the film, there's a scene where a car pulls up on a shitty night and there's this big, scary house on a hill and at the top of the building is a single light in a window with a shadowy figure looking down. As I pulled the ambulance up at the address we'd been given, I looked up through the rain towards the multi-storey house on the hill and there was a single lit window and a shadowy figure looking out.

I turned to my partner and said: 'Bro, it's Norman Bates. We're fucked.'

The dispatcher had told us that there was an 80-year-old who had collapsed; we had to get him to hospital. We loaded up our stair-chair, which was what we used to get people out of buildings if they couldn't walk and it wasn't practical to use a stretcher. Oxygen, defibrillator — everything we'd possibly need — we grabbed hold of it and headed towards the house.

The notes said the front door didn't work and we were to go into the garage via a roller door. So I pulled it up and in the dark looked around for an internal door. Then we heard a loud noise — *clang, clang, clang* — coming from behind a curtain. The noise stopped, a hand pulled the curtain aside, and a man who looked like Igor in the *Frankenstein* films stepped out of an old elevator. It was the patient's son.

'There's only enough room for two, so youse go up and I'll wait down here,' he said in a squeaky, rasping voice. 'There's no light in there, it's pitch-black, but you're perfectly safe.' *Oh, fuck*, I thought to myself.

We squeezed into the lift with the stair-chair and our equipment, 'Igor' closed the curtain and the grille door, and the elevator started to rattle and shake its way up. I couldn't see my hand in front of me, and the noise was a real racket. 'We're going to die in this elevator,' I said to my partner. He'd gone completely silent.

Eventually, the shaking and shuddering stopped and the door opened. The patient's grandson was waiting for us. The first thing that hit us was a rank smell, one that made you wish you could hold your breath until you got outside again. But that wasn't going to be possible. The grandson led us to the patient, who must have been lying on his bed for a long, long time. He had long, curly nails and long, matted hair, and we had to almost peel him off the bed to sit him up.

After we checked him out, we told him he needed to go to hospital. He wasn't keen, but after twenty minutes of cajoling we convinced him to get on the chair. We pushed him back towards the elevator. By that stage, I'd somehow adjusted to the environment and could finally take things in. The place was a mess; there wasn't much cleaning going on by any of the three men apparently living here. Then I noticed there were hundreds and hundreds of dolls, all around the place — from small ones to huge ones, half my size. Everywhere. I asked who the dolls belonged to, and the grandson said: 'They're Mum's.' There was no sign of her anywhere in the house.

My partner hadn't said a word since we got to the house. But when we got to the lift, to go back down to the ambulance, a thought came into my head: *Only two of us can get in the lift. Someone's going to have to stay here while the other one takes the patient down.* As the old man was my patient, it meant my partner was going to have to wait at the top. I was a bit worried he'd lose it. So I figured I needed to break the ice.

I put my hand on his shoulder and quietly said: 'It's okay, bro, you're safe. Nothing's going to happen to you.'

And he said: 'Why's that?'

'Because in these types of movies, it's always the black guy who gets it first.' I hopped in the elevator, pushed the patient in, and my plan must have worked because my partner had a smile on his face.

That was one of the most out-of-it jobs I ever went to.

+ + +

Another aspect of ambulance work I enjoyed was interacting with people from all walks of life. And because of the life I'd led, I could feel comfortable in just about any situation.

One day we had a call-out to a part of Auckland that was well known as the area of a certain gang. It didn't matter at all to me — all we were doing was responding to a call for help. We had our lights and sirens on; the job was a code red, a child with a history of asthma who was experiencing shortness of breath. Asthma is an obstruction of the airways, caused by inflammation. Some people have mild cases, and all they need is a puff on an inhaler and they're okay again. But for others it can be life-threatening. This girl had previously been admitted to hospital with serious asthma attacks, so this was a real emergency.

We pulled up to the house, went to the door, and the guy who opened it had a patch on his back. No big deal to me, because I knew the street, though my partner was worried about going in. 'It's okay, we're sweet,' I told her.

I said to the guy: 'Oh, bro, is your daughter's asthma kicking up?'

He said, 'Yeah, bro, come in, please.' Straight away I could see that in that moment, he wasn't a gangster — he was just a concerned father worried about his daughter, like anyone else would be.

We went inside, and immediately assessed that while she was struggling for breath, she was doing okay in the circumstances. I could hear her wheezing — it's when you *don't* hear any sound that you really have to worry. It's one of the signs we look for; another one is how hard they're using all their other muscles to breathe, and how tired and drawn they look.

I could see that this girl was at the start of her attack; the whānau had called us early, which was great. We put a nebuliser on her; a mask attached to a small machine that helps get medicine and oxygen into a patient's lungs. Her breathing started to improve immediately. Even so, we needed to get her to hospital for monitoring. I explained to the dad what was happening, and that she was going to be okay.

He was happy. But not long after he realised his daughter was safe, he turned back into a gangster. As we were getting ready to leave, his face creased into a snarl and he said: 'You took your fucking time getting here, didn't you?'

I said: 'What?'

'You fucking heard me,' he said.

I looked straight at him and said: 'Bro, we just fucking saved your daughter's life. Fuck up, eh?'

It probably wasn't the response he was expecting from an ambulance officer, and he went: 'Oh, yeah, true. Okay, bro.'

He needed that short, sharp shock to bring him back to the reality of what was going on. But I guess you needed to have had experience of his world to know that. I wondered what it would have been like if someone who didn't know that was sent to the job. Whether the police would have been called; whether the crew would have even held off going into the house in the first place without a police escort, worried about their own safety. It's good that people think of their own safety. But a delay in getting to the girl might have cost her her life.

+ + +

There was another job where who I was, where I came from, had a direct impact on a situation. But this one was quite funny.

We got called out to a party which had gone completely sideways. There was a riot going on in the street — like an actual riot, where kids were throwing bottles at cops with shields and batons. In the middle of all that, a pregnant woman had fallen over.

Pulling up, I spotted her lying on the ground by a letter box. I went over to her, knelt down and started talking with her, finding out what was going on. All the while, bottles were flying overhead and there was yelling and screaming. It was mayhem.

It turned out she'd felt dizzy and had ended up lying down on the ground. She was 36 weeks pregnant. 'Okay, we'll check you out and get you to hospital,' I told her. I was operating by the light of a streetlamp, just concentrating on doing my job amidst the melee.

But then I noticed there was a bit of a lull, and some chattering going on. A Māori boy came hurrying towards me, crouched down low but moving swiftly. 'Hey, bro,' he said when he got close to us. 'None of the bottles are hurting you, are they?'

'Nah,' I told him, 'they're not coming in our direction.'

'Okay, sweet,' he said, then ran back to his mates and the riot resumed. I think an instruction went out: 'Don't throw anything over there — he's a Māori paramedic.'

Being Māori paid off for me that night, but there were plenty of occasions during my career as a paramedic where the opposite was true. And sometimes it was shocking to hear where the racist crap came from.

Chapter 18

And Then She Died

Working on an ambulance, racing around the city, doing lots of crazy shit, experiencing the adrenaline rush of resuscitating someone; sometimes it felt like being on the most intoxicating drug. It could be so intense, a twelve-hour shift of so many extremes — literally life and death — and I'd get a high out of it, feeling really pumped.

I'd chase the high — do a resuss, take the patient to hospital, clean up the truck, then turn to my partner and say, 'Are we good?'

'Yeah, we're good — let's go.' We'd hit the button to let comms know we were ready for the next job. And off we'd go, hungry for another high.

On resuss jobs you were fighting for someone's life; whether they lived or died could be in your hands. So despite the high of a successful outcome, it was heavy and super-stressful. It was also physically exhausting: you'd be doing CPR on someone, keeping their heart pumping, and sweat would be pouring off you, your body aching, but you just had to keep going. It took its toll, both mentally and physically. One day I had four resuss jobs, and that was my first shift in a four-day stretch. I went home shattered, with three more twelve-hour shifts ahead of me. It was easy for paramedics to burn out without them even knowing. A lot of the older guys were in that state, but it was the only thing they knew so they just kept going.

Another reason it was intense was you were constantly being thrust into the most intimate, heartbreaking whānau moments; people losing their parents, children, siblings, and you were the one who had to be there for them, take charge and take care of them, too.

There was one call-out I remember very clearly, a Rarotongan whānau. A family member had collapsed and we were called out, lights and sirens. When we arrived we immediately got to work, but it was clear he had passed away already. I was with an intensive-care paramedic (ICP) who had the authority to provide higher-level care such as intubating the patient — inserting a tube to keep the airways open and get air to the lungs — but not even those options were going to bring him back.

I spoke with the patient's eldest daughter, explaining that he had passed, and she was accepting of the situation. So I went to the ambulance to get the paperwork we had to fill out for a death. By the time I got back inside, the ICP had restarted resuss work even though, clinically, it was hopeless. The youngest daughter had become upset, saying we couldn't let her father go — his other kids and grandkids were coming so he needed to be kept alive to see them to say goodbye.

I spoke to the eldest daughter again. 'He's passed away, he's gone,' I said to her.

'Yes, but my sister wants us to keep trying.'

I turned to the youngest sister and called out her name.

'What?' she almost snapped back at me.

'Kua mate,' I said. Which means 'He's died.'

With those words, she accepted it. She put her head down, and we stopped the resuss. We prepared her father to look as best as he could for when the rest of the whānau arrived. When they did, I said a karakia for the whānau and did a mihi to them all, and we left. In that most painful of moments, I had been able to help them process what had happened to their father and accept that he had passed. It was a privilege to have had that opportunity to help. At a time of deep sorrow and grief, it was beautiful.

+ + +

So the thing about being a paramedic was, I loved the job but I hated working there. Not only did I have to put up with quips and questions about the manslaughter case, but there were also instances of straight-out bias and racism. As an institution it was predominantly Pākehā, and there was a sense of entitlement along with a blatant disregard for what was inappropriate when I worked there.

Some managers didn't even care when they said things in front of total strangers. One night I was doing a story with some journalists about my Waitangi Tribunal claim. They were filming me at an ambulance station when a manager noticed us. We'd been given permission to be there, so that wasn't a problem. But he came over and said to the crew, 'Oh, why are you here?'

I told him they were filming me.

'Why are they filming you?'

I told him it was because I'd taken a claim against institutional racism in the police.

He turned to the crew and said, 'Bloody Māoris.' He had no idea who the crew was, he didn't know if the camera was rolling or not — but he didn't seem to care. He tried to make out it was a joke, keeping on talking other rubbish, but we were all just gobsmacked. It was just so blatant, and for him to have said that in front of strangers, it was obvious he couldn't see any problem with it.

And it wasn't the only time I saw examples where the underlying culture and toxicity shone through. Another time I'd been called to a meeting after a complaint about me — I'll come back to that. I'd asked my lawyer to come with me for backup. We were sitting down with one of the managers, waiting for another staff member, and the manager said, 'Oh, she'll come waddling over as soon as she can.'

My lawyer assumed that the woman must have been pregnant, but in fact she was just a big woman and he was being blatantly offensive about her weight. This manager didn't know my lawyer, but he just didn't care that he thought it was okay to be offensive in front of her about one of his own team members. It was so unprofessional and completely disgusting.

Back to the complaint . . . one of the people I'd been partnered up with on a shift had alleged that while we were on a lights and sirens call, I'd been leaning out the window at some traffic lights, swearing at and abusing motorists who wouldn't get out of the way. The manager asked me what I had to say for myself.

I asked him: 'How many times during a lights and sirens call-out have you had your window down, let alone been hanging out the window?' The answer was never — no one ever did, because the siren was so loud it would deafen you. You always kept the window closed tight.

'So I can't have been hanging out the window because we never put our windows down — she's lying,' I said.

The manager didn't back down. Instead, he tried to tell me what he thought my partner had really meant to say — in other words, making up a different scenario. He disregarded what she'd written in her statement and just invented some other facts. It was outrageous.

Considering that was the sort of shit that happened in front of other people, imagine what happened when it was just me there? Even though I loved the job, it was so difficult to get up and go to work each day dreading what was going to be said or complained about next.

+ + +

In the end, though, the reason I decided to change direction again wasn't to do with that stuff and nonsense. It was a call-out on the North Shore.

As we headed there, we learned there was a woman in her eighties who was suffering severe respiratory distress. When we walked in, we saw she was what we call 'tripodding': sitting on the edge of a chair, leaning forward with her hands on her knees, using all the muscles in her body to try to breathe. This 'tripod' position is something people do when they are having real trouble breathing. And she was having extreme difficulty.

Unlike that asthma case with the young girl and the father who was in a gang, this time I couldn't hear any wheezing; her body was heaving up and down but there was no sound. She looked fatigued. I knelt beside her, took hold of her wrist and said, 'Love, tell me why I'm here today.'

She replied, 'I. Can't. Breathe.' One word per breath. Her wrist was cold and wet and I couldn't feel a radial pulse.

'Bro,' I said to my partner, 'she's status one, go get a stretcher — she doesn't need us, she needs a hospital.' He rushed out to the ambulance, and I started doing what I could to help her and reassure her. I put an oxygen mask on her face, a blood pressure cuff on her arm and grabbed a stethoscope to listen to her lungs. I said to her, 'This is going to be a bit tight on your arm for a second.' I turned a little to have a listen to the lungs, and she stared at me then fell back into the couch. She was having a cardiac arrest.

I put her on the floor and immediately began compressions on her chest, pumping her heart for her. My partner came in and grabbed the defibrillator, a machine used to shock the heart, in the hope it would save her life.

Now, there are only two heartbeat rhythms you can shock: VT or VF. But her heartbeat was showing a sinus rhythm, a normal rhythm, something you or I would have. I thought, *Bullshit.* I felt for the carotid pulse in her neck and there was none.

What we were dealing was something called 'pulseless electrical activity' (PEA). It looks like there's a heartbeat, but there's actually no pulse. The heart relies on electrical signals to work. The signal starts at the top right, in the sinoatrial node, where a cluster of cells creates an electrical current. As the current goes around the top of the heart to the bottom, it causes a contraction. In a normal heart, this all happens seamlessly — conduction, contraction, conduction, contraction. The heart beats normally and blood is pumped around the body. In this case, our patient had conduction but no contraction.

We were in full-on resuss mode, desperately fighting for this woman's life. In the back of my mind I knew it was all on us; it was a busy day so there was no backup coming. The defibrillator couldn't help — PEA is an 'unshockable' condition. So the compressions on her heart were the only thing keeping the blood pumping around her body.

I thought back to my training and university and recalled that there were nine things that could cause PEA, known as the 'Five Hs and Four Ts'. I was ticking them off in my head, working through to the most likely. We had been taught a few interventions that could help, but there were some things only an advanced paramedic was licensed to do. One of these involved intubation, inserting a tube down the throat. Although I'd graduated as an advanced paramedic and had had the opportunity to perform an intubation in hospital, I was unable to do it in the field.

Another possible action was emergency treatment for pericarditis, inflammation of the heart, which she had a history of. This involves inserting a long needle filled with saline solution under the ribs, pushing all the way up towards the shoulder. If you encounter resistance, that's the fluid-filled sac called the pericardium — bubbles will appear in the saline, and it will turn a different colour. With pericarditis, the pericardium is inflamed and it squeezes the heart, eventually preventing it from contracting. If you get the needle in the right place, you can suck all the shit out and the heart can start pumping again.

So, there were two things that could possibly help — but we didn't have the equipment to do them. And even if we did have the gear, we weren't licensed to do them and would have lost our jobs for acting outside of our authority.

With zero likelihood of any backup coming, I knew that as soon as I stopped moving her heart for her, that would be it: she'd be dead.

We kept doing our compressions; got an intravenous line in; ran fluids; pushed drugs; and did our two-minute checks. After about 30 minutes of hard, physical effort, with sweat dripping off us as we took turns pressing down on her heart, we had to face the inevitable. The longer we went on, the less effective our compressions became because of our own fatigue. There was no way she was coming back. As soon as we stopped, she was gone.

I looked at my partner and said, 'Are you good?'

'Yeah,' he said, 'I'm good.' It was the most euphemistic way of saying, 'Are we going to let this woman die now?' That was the harsh reality.

He'd wanted to call it ten minutes earlier, but had kept going because I'd kept going. That's what happens: hanging on to hope. But all hope had gone. We stopped the compressions, the adrenaline dissipated, she flatlined, and we called time of death.

Her husband had been there the whole time, watching all the lengths we went to, seeing how hard we were trying to save his wife's life, and he was appreciative. But when I left that job, I felt like I'd ripped her off. I did not have the necessary expertise to save her; I had reached the limit of what I could do. Don't get me wrong: I'm not God and I knew that people were going to die in my care. Yet something about this case tipped things for me. I wanted to give people the best possible outcome I could give them. And for her, I hadn't. I needed to do something.

The next day, I applied for medical school. I was determined to make a difference, to strive for the best I could be. Exactly what shape that would take, what kind of doctor I wanted to be, I didn't exactly know. But I'd made up my mind, just as I had when I'd stared out at the blue sky through the prison window as a teenager and instinctively knew there was another way; just as I had when I'd hopped on a plane to Sydney with nothing more than a desire to make a new life; just as I had when I'd posted my patch back to the motorcycle club in Adelaide.

And just as had been the case my whole life, I was not going to let my past hold me back; and neither was I going to let others' impressions of me throw me from my path.

+ + +

Of course, deciding you want to go to medical school and getting in to medical school are two different things. It's like *Mastermind* meets *The Hunger Games* just to get in the door.

There are two medical schools in Aotearoa: Auckland and Otago. I wanted to go to Auckland because it was home, and I was hoping to be able to do some part-time work on the ambulances. Getting in to Auckland is super-competitive, but I backed myself and went for it.

Like everyone, I had to do the UMAT — the Undergraduate Medicine and Health Sciences Admission Test — which assessed critical thinking, problem solving and empathy. (UMAT has since been replaced by a new test.) It was a three-hour test where all sorts of problems and scenarios were laid out and you had to give the 'right' answer. I later heard that the answers were partly based on what a pool of 500 people thought, which made me wonder: *What happens if you don't think like the majority of other people? And what's wrong with that?*

Anyway, I sat the test, did okay and got an interview. Fingers crossed. But then I got a letter saying I'd missed out. But hey, impediments like that had never stopped me before. I applied again to Auckland the next year . . . and I missed out again.

You're only allowed to apply to Auckland twice, so that

was my hopes of staying home dashed. But it hadn't killed my ambition and desire to be a doctor. So, I had another shot via Otago. I applied as a post-graduate student because I had my paramedicine degree, and they invited me to come down for the first year, which involved studying a broad bunch of papers with the aim of doing well enough to make it into the second year.

I'd never been to Dunedin before, so my cousin and I decided to do a road trip. I had a beaten-up old Toyota and we drove down the country. It was after the Kaikōura earthquakes so State Highway 1 at the top of the South Island was munted, meaning we had to take a huge detour. We didn't care; it was an experience.

About 150 kilometres from Dunedin, we stopped at a beach with some pizzas and a box of beers and stayed the night. It felt like a final taste of freedom before the tough year ahead of me began. Next morning I dropped my cousin at the airport to fly back to Auckland, then went into town to get settled.

I stayed with a fellow paramedic and her super-smart dog, Clancy, in south Dunedin, which was just a short drive from my lectures. I hadn't been in a lecture theatre for ages and had to work hard to get my head around the core papers we had to do in that first year — chemistry, physics, epidemiology and microbiology. I took extra classes because I didn't understand half the stuff. Physics nearly broke me: 'You're a detective and you turn up to a house where someone has drowned in a 2m pool. When you're walking towards the pool, where are you standing when you can first see the body on the bottom of the pool?' *Um, what the fuck?*

During the first year there were about 4000 students. Not all of them wanted to go on to study medicine, but the stakes were still high — only about 300 were going to get through. As one of 50 post-grad students, my chances were higher because they were going to take ten of us. But even so I knew I had to nail it in my final exams.

In the end, I did well — but I knew it wasn't good enough. The people I was competing against were super-smart. And so it proved: I missed out for a third time.

I went back to Auckland to think about my future. Was I having doubts about whether I could make it? You don't go through what I've been through in my life just to give up easily. I've been thoroughly conditioned to knock-backs and challenges; I know how to get back up. Every time.

I knew there had to be a way. There just *had* to be.

Chapter 19

A Shock Diagnosis

Perhaps it shouldn't have been a surprise that I didn't do as well as I'd hoped in my final exams that first year at Otago. The build-up had not exactly gone smoothly.

First, there was the tension of knowing there was a lot riding on it, with so many students competing for so few places at the medical school the following year. Around this time, I was also being pressured into resitting my practising certificate so I could keep working on the ambulances in Auckland over the summer break.

Earlier in the year I'd asked if I could do the test in Dunedin, but that was declined; and then, as the exams loomed, I asked if I could postpone until afterwards since there was so much riding on them and I really didn't want to be distracted. But the bosses wouldn't back down and my certification lapsed. That was one of the things I had to sort out over summer — I took them to mediation. I can't say much because of confidentiality requirements; suffice it to say I was back working on the ambulances not long afterwards.

So, yeah, given all that was going on, it perhaps wasn't a huge surprise when my exam results weren't quite good enough.

Being able to work on the ambulances was useful while I figured out my next steps. I was determined to carry on with medical studies somehow. I looked at my options, and saw that Otago had another pathway called the alternative category. The aim was to attract a range of academically suitable applicants with broad life experience, skills and perspectives. Makes sense, right? Having people who come from all walks of life is better than having cookie-cutter, one-size-fits-all doctors.

There were strict criteria to meet, and a stipulation that this would be a one-shot chance. *Fuck it*, I thought, *I'm going for it.* Applications opened in March but didn't close until May. So once I'd sent off my application, I just tried to get on with work and not think about it too much.

Then, one day, I got an email inviting me down for an interview. They said they could see I'd studied hard and my grades showed I was capable, so they were prepared to give me an opportunity to convince them I deserved a spot via the alternative category.

Ahead of the interview, I had to write a letter setting out my case. It felt like the most important words I was ever going to have to write in my life. I poured my heart into it, explaining my life, the things I'd been through, and why there needed to be people like me in medicine. And then I flew down to Dunedin, nervous as hell, knowing my future depended on it.

I fronted up to a panel of three people, and from the get-go I could tell I had a decent shot. One panel member kept saying he'd never seen anyone with my background apply for medicine. With the questions he asked, and the comments he made, I felt hopeful. Still, the decision was in others' hands. I'd done all I could. Now it was up to them.

I knew from experience that in those situations, it paid to try to put it out of mind, to try not to worry about it. I headed back to work, back to the ambulances.

And one day, *ping*, an email arrived. 'Congratulations,' it read. I was being offered a chance to study medicine at Otago University, starting in 2019. *Fuck, yes!* After so many attempts, so many rejections, I was going to study to become a doctor. The kid who had dropped out of school, whose enthusiasm for the classroom had been shoved and beaten out of him.

Had my goal ever seemed like it was slipping from my grasp? Maybe. Had I ever considered giving up? Never. Had I even once had an expectation that I somehow deserved to have it delivered to me? No way.

It had been a test of patience. But if there's one thing you learn when you're forced to sit for hours on end on your own in your bedroom as a kid, or when you get sentenced to prison and you're confronted with the mundanity of a routine you cannot escape, it's patience. And, finally, that patience had been rewarded.

+ + +

After I found out I'd been accepted to Otago, I decided to shout myself an overseas trip. I had a bit of money saved, and some leave owing, and I realised I was about to become a poor student again — and a busy one at that. I wouldn't get another chance for a proper break for years. I wanted to go somewhere they hardly spoke English and where I could experience another culture. So I chose to go to India, a country that intrigued me and seemed to tick all the boxes for the types of experiences I wanted to have.

I stepped off the plane in Mumbai, a huge, smelly, noisy, vibrant city. And I fucking loved it. I had an itinerary, but I thought, *Nah, fuck this.* I ripped it up, then hooked up to the airport internet and searched for the slums of Mumbai. I found backpackers' accommodation about a kilometre away from the entrance, took a crazy taxi ride to get there, and got my bearings sorted.

The next morning, I woke up early to the sound of the call to prayer from a nearby mosque. I knew exactly what I wanted to do. After breakfast I checked out and walked straight to the slums. The next three nights, I slept under a bridge in one of the poorest parts of the city. By day I wandered around, just taking everything in, interacting with people, seeing how they lived. It was unbelievable. These people showed me the value of simplicity, and I could relate to their single-mindedness and determination to survive. Each day was about finding some food for their family, finding some work, and doing whatever they could to support each other.

After those three nights, I experienced the culture shock of India's vast disparity. I walked out of the slum, and within 100 metres of the exit was a massive, sparkling mall. I withdrew some money at a cash machine, found a shower and had a meal at a flash restaurant — I'd deliberately not eaten while I was in the slum to avoid getting sick.

Then I went back to the slums for another three days. It was remarkable.

After my stay in Mumbai, I flew to Rajasthan for some sightseeing, then to Goa, the party town. It had been colonised by the Portuguese, who introduced wine. Unlike the rest of India where there was hardly any alcohol, Goa was soaked in it. I stayed on the beach for ten days, getting shit-faced every day.

It was my last blow-out before the most intense work of my life began.

+ + +

Before I headed back to Dunedin, I thought, *If I'm going to be a doctor, I need a doctor car*. So I took out a loan and I bought a Lexus. Yes, a Lexus. I cruised down the country in this flash-as car and it was fucking cool.

Then reality hit: once I got to Dunedin, I didn't have anywhere to stay. So for two nights I lived in my car — two nights in this car I'd bought thinking I was so damn flash. Ha!

Eventually I found a house north of the city in the hill suburb of Normanby, flatting with two guys: the owner, who worked on a farm, and an anaesthetic technician from England who was also a brilliant cook. I kept telling him he should be a chef.

One of the reasons I moved in with them was because the environment was more mature than a lot of Dunedin flats. We'd have cups of tea and a chat rather than beers and raging parties. It was worth it, even if the place was so cold in winter. While it had a great heater in the lounge where it would be toasty and warm, in my bedroom it was often below freezing. I'd have as many layers of clothes on me as I could get on, and all the blankets piled up, and I'd still be shivering. But it was a small price to pay because the place was awesome, and just what I needed as a haven in which to knuckle down and study.

Which was just as well, because there was *so much* study to do. Information came roaring towards me like it was shooting out of a fire hose. Relentless, intense, overwhelming. I was drowning in it. Lecture after tutorial after lecture after tutorial. But I was loving it. Unlike that first year studying core papers, this was all focused towards medicine — no more questions about light refraction and swimming pools.

We each got assigned a cadaver to help us understand anatomy. Every year, people bequeath their bodies to the medical school. I got a 93-year-old man; you don't get his name or anything. But I gave him a name and I'd address him each time, and then at the end of the session I'd say, 'Thank you for allowing me to learn.' It was an amazing part of our studies, and I'll be forever grateful to those who donated. It was just so good to be able to have that practical learning experience: to be taught about muscles or tendons or different layers of the fascia, and then to go and find them and see them for yourself.

Every single moment I had I was desperate to learn, spending hour after hour hitting the books, studying in the library. But while I was avoiding the social aspect of life as an Otago student, I was still enjoying the camaraderie. It had a different vibe to the first year where thousands of people were competing for so few spots. This was less about competition and more about making sure everyone made it through.

Which was just as well. The competition in that first year was madness; people would do whatever it took to get ahead. Once, a tutor was busted for teaching the wrong information to deliberately disadvantage other students. Another time, a student was in the library and got up to go to the toilet, leaving their laptop on the table. Someone stole it and threw it in the river. Shit like that was not uncommon. It was wild. But when you've been in environments where staring down a rival might mean the difference between life and death, I might not have enjoyed it but I wasn't exactly fazed.

I was lucky, too, that through the university's Māori programme I'd met a lot of other Māori students and it was amazing to be a part of that; whanaungatanga and kotahitanga at its best. Still, in the second year, it was good not to have any more of that bullshit hyper-competitiveness from some people. I was keen to knuckle down, get on with it, and avoid all unnecessary distractions.

But me being me, it was probably not surprising that another curveball hit just as I was preparing for my final exams.

I was diagnosed with a brain tumour.

+ + +

I'd gone to see a doctor at the university GP clinic about a couple of issues, nothing major. I mentioned that I had problems sleeping, decreased energy, things like that. We'd finished the consultation and I was getting ready to leave, and she said: 'Is that all?'

And I said: 'Well, actually, I've had erectile dysfunction for years now.' I'd never mentioned it to anyone before. I'd first noticed it when I was in Australia, so it was an issue that went back a long, long time — more than a decade.

When I was in the bikie club, it turned out to be an advantage of sorts. Towards the end of my time with the club, when I felt like there were people out to set me up, women would be put in front of me in what were obviously honey-trap situations. But because I couldn't get it up, it was a useless tactic to try on me.

Over the years, when I'd thought about why I had erectile dysfunction, I'd rationalised it in a couple of ways. First I thought back to my fucked-up life and the fact I'd endured so much abuse, including sexual abuse. And then, it came on after my marriage ended so I'd always assumed it could be tied up with that, too. My marriage was such a toxic relationship — me as much as her — that I figured there must have been some consequences.

Certainly, it had impacted my relationships with women: I didn't trust anyone and wouldn't let anyone get close to me.

But in the GP's clinic that day, the doctor said: 'Okay, I'm going to get some blood tests done.' A couple of days later she asked me to come in to the clinic. She was concerned about the levels of a hormone called prolactin. A normal level would be around 400 micrograms per litre — mine came back at about 18,000. Prolactin, along with other hormones, is produced in the small gland in the brain called the pituitary. But when you excrete more of it — and in my case much more of it — then it causes complications such as decreased energy, lowered libido and, yep, erectile dysfunction.

I got sent for an MRI and it showed a tumour. It wasn't huge, in fact the gland was only about 1 centimetre larger than normal. A bit like me: unassuming but very productive. It was called a prolactinoma, a benign tumour on the pituitary gland. It could be treated with a drug called cabergoline, which I was started on. It came with some side effects that weren't exactly helpful as I studied for my finals: low blood pressure, constipation, and the fact that after years of having no erections, suddenly I was . . . which was a bit distracting. With everything that was going on, honestly I thought I'd bombed the exams.

But when I got my results back, I'd passed. Not by much, but I'd passed. I was happy with that, given the complication of being diagnosed with a brain tumour.

\+ + +

In my next year, I decided, *You know, I haven't tasted proper student life, ever. I'm going to have a bit of fun this year.* So I went to a few parties and spent a few days at the library hungover. In other words, I got to enjoy a bit of the typical Otago experience.

There's a photo I've got as the screensaver on my phone of a bunch of fellow Māori and Pasifika students after a 'flat crawl'. It's like a pub crawl except it's around half a dozen flats, and you go drinking from place to place. After one flat crawl where we'd all dressed up as nineties hoods we all posed for this photo. I crack up every time I look at it.

I didn't get into any kind of sexual relationship; I found it awkward. But hanging with the boys and getting shit-faced every now and again was cool.

Of course, since it was 2020, there weren't as many opportunities to catch up and socialise with people as normal. Thanks, Covid. The arrival of a global pandemic was not exactly conducive to a smooth year. All our classes went online, via Zoom. When the first lockdown happened, suddenly we were all stuck at home, in our bubbles. Some people went a bit crazy, but I'd experienced being confined to a small space plenty of times. So this was nothing. I just chilled in the flat and got on with things. Study, go out for a run (close to home, of course), eat delicious food cooked by a guy who could easily be a chef . . . it wasn't a bad routine. And the good thing about having lectures online was I could rewind them and listen to tricky bits again.

As the end of the year approached, we had a decision to make. At Otago, the fourth to sixth years are taught at campuses attached to hospitals in Dunedin, Christchurch and Wellington. We had to choose our preferred location.

I wanted to go to Wellington for a couple of reasons: it was in the same island as Auckland, my home, so that would be easier to drive to; and the Waitangi Tribunal claim I'd made was approaching the stage where there would be hearings, which were going to be in Wellington. So it made sense. Wellington was also the least popular choice for some reason, which meant I got my preference.

It was time to start a new life in the capital, as well as embarking on the final straight of my studies; albeit a straight that was three years long. I was really looking forward to this phase: less about learning from books and more about learning how to deal with sick people in practice. And that, I've gotta say, was my jam.

I pointed my Lexus towards Wellington and drove.

Chapter 20

Change in My Hands

Something big happened when I moved to Wellington. I changed my name. Or, I should say, I changed my name *back* — back to what it was when I was born, before I was given my stepfather's surname. It was important to me to reclaim my name so that when I graduated as a doctor, I would do so as Timoti Te Moke.

There were a few other things that were changing in my life as well. When I was in Dunedin I'd started exercising and I wanted to keep that going, so one of the first things I did once I'd settled into Wellington, in a flat not far from the hospital, was find a gym. I'd had a bit of an epiphany when I'd begun studying medicine: that I should be looking after myself a bit more. As a doctor, I thought, it would be harder to get buy-in from patients

I needed to talk to about making better life choices if I looked like I'd eaten all the pies myself. So I hit the gym, ate healthier and started shedding weight, about 35 kilograms. It made me feel so much better and I was determined to keep up my healthy ways. Of course, finally being treated for the brain tumour made a difference, too, especially to my energy levels.

In Wellington there was a small gym at the hospital which only cost a dollar a day; perfect for a poor student, so I'd rock up there. My routine became: go to tutorials in the morning, head to the hospital for time on the wards, go to the library to do some study, hit the gym, and go home. Rinse and repeat, day after day. I was on a mission. Everyone who goes to med school is, but mine was a bit different. I'd noticed that some of the younger students felt the pressure a lot; I guess you'd call it the pressure of expectation. For some of them, the 'prestige' of being a medical student carried its own stress. Their parents were proud of them, their friends looked up to them. When they were finding it tough — like we all did from time to time — that was an extra burden to carry. I didn't have that pressure. The way I saw it, there was no expectation on me; at least, in that way. I wasn't there because anybody was pushing me. I was doing this on my own terms.

However, I did go and see a psychologist a couple of times about the pressure I was putting on myself. I'd been thinking about the importance of realising my potential; getting my head around what it was I trying to achieve, the pathway I was on. I felt: *I can't fail. This must happen, this must work out — no one has come from my part of the world, been through what I have, to get here. I have to make it; I have to make it.* With those thoughts swirling around my head, it was good to sit down and talk with the psychologist about them; cathartic even. I needed to make some sense of what I was thinking and feeling, and make it a positive force rather than let it turn into a burden.

Getting my headspace sorted was important because I had plenty of work to do. These three years at Otago University's Wellington campus, doing more hands-on learning in hospital, would determine my future. Now there was more emphasis on dealing with patients and less on textbooks (though there were still piles of those to study), I began to feel more comfortable. Years of working on the ambulances had made me confident dealing with people who were unwell, injured or distressed.

Maybe I was a bit too confident; at least, that's what my supervisors thought. The idea was that they would slowly and carefully introduce us students into working with patients. I found it hard because I already knew how to talk with people, to help them, and I had so much experience at it. I'd constantly be held back, urged to slow down. Faced with someone in a clinical situation, our supervisors would be asking: 'Why is this happening? Why is that happening?' I'd be chafing at the bit, thinking: *I don't know the answer you want — but I know what to do in this situation, so just let me do it.*

But the reins were being held tightly, so I had to learn to not let my instincts take over, to just slow down and follow the process we were expected to follow, and to soak up all the knowledge we were being taught.

Part of the process of learning to be a doctor was being exposed to all the different fields, getting a taste of them and starting to get an early feel for where we might like to end up in a few years' time — after a mountain-sized pile of more training and learning. Some of the rotations I knew virtually straight away weren't for me; paediatrics and psych were two of those. With obstetrics and gynaecology, I found the work itself really interesting but I felt like a dick explaining women's own problems to them: 'This is what you've got, and this is why you're feeling this way.' Nah, not for me.

I enjoyed my surgical runs at Wellington Hospital. Picking up a scalpel seemed to come naturally. There were some good people to learn off, too. I got on well with one of the senior medical officers (SMOs) in Wellington, especially because we were both *Star Wars* fans. One time, in surgery, he was shepherding a registrar through a procedure and the registrar was having a bit of difficulty. Out of the blue I said: 'Do. Or do not. There is no try.' It's a famous quote from the character Yoda in *The Empire Strikes Back*. The SMO cracked up laughing.

I am planning on becoming an intensivist — a specialist who works in ICU. Almost all patients that come to ICU have undergone some sort of surgery to keep them alive, and it is that aspect of surgery that fascinates me. For example, during a bowel operation in Wellington, the surgeon asked me to get my hands inside the patient to hold up the bowel so they could see underneath it with a camera. There I was, with my hands gently cradling someone's bowel, contributing to the work of a team of sharp-minded experts. I looked up at the screen in the theatre and was just struck by the moment — a realisation of how much my life and circumstances had changed.

It was unreal. A task and a place I could never have imagined in my wildest dreams during all those years when opportunity and a sense of my contribution to society being valued were non-existent; a time when society preferred I be locked up and treated with disdain.

+ + +

At the end of the six-week surgical placement in my fifth year, just as with other blocks that year, we had an assessment on our second-to-last day. It seemed to go well, and so I celebrated with another student. When I say celebrated . . . we got shit-faced. Beers, tequila . . . we gave everything a good crack.

Sometime during the night we remembered we had baking to do. It was traditional to take some baking in to the team as a thank you. Except we weren't in any shape to be cooking. But there we were in the kitchen, chucking flour and sugar and everything else around. Actually, some of it didn't make it into the right bowls and tins because we forgot some of the ingredients.

The next day, I turned up with the biggest hangover I'd ever had, with sad-looking biscuits and stuff, saying, 'Um, sorry, it doesn't look that good and it's missing a few things, but it tastes alright . . .' Everyone cracked up and they seemed to enjoy it.

They seemed to understand about my hangover, too, because they let me hang out at the back during our ward runs as I tried to ignore my thumping headache and queasy stomach.

+ + +

As I made my way through medical school, people started to learn about my background and I had opportunities to tell my story, both formally and informally. In my fifth year, I got asked to go down to Dunedin to talk to a conference for theatre staff. I put a lot of work into it, but I was still blown away when I got paid $1500 on top of being flown down and put up in a hotel. (The flip side was that I flew back and went straight to an exam, which I failed; but it worked out okay because I was allowed to resit it and passed fine.)

I was discovering that my story had value. And not just monetary value — much more than that. It was something I could use to help people. The path I'd walked to get here had given me experiences no one else had. I was unique.

One day I was starting a day shift on my rotation in the intensive care ward. The night-shift registrar was handing over to the day staff and he mentioned a patient who'd come in overnight. His head went down and his shoulders slumped. *What was going on here?* The registrar described the patient: a fifteen-year-old boy who'd had a car accident a few years ago and suffered a severe head injury. Ever since then he'd had seizures, and each time he did he'd be back in hospital. By now, everyone (apart from me) knew who he was talking about. Everyone's head went down and everyone's shoulders slumped.

Then he said the kid's name, and I figured out why everyone's heads had gone down. The kid had the same name as a guy who'd founded a gang chapter in south Auckland. I didn't know his namesake personally, but I'd grown up with plenty of people who did.

The registrar explained that the kid was going to be brought on to the ward to be extubated — which is what happens when someone who has been intubated is ready to start breathing for themselves. During intubation a tube is put down their throat, and a machine then breathes for them. When they're ready for the tube to be removed, the sedation gets switched off and as they start coming around, the tube gets pulled out.

I asked if I could help with the extubation. 'Sure,' I was told, like I was asking to do something crazy.

I went into the cubicle and there's the boy, his mother, his older brother, and two small nurses who were shitting themselves. There were also about six security staff.

I said to the security guys: 'It's all good, you don't need to be here.'

'We've got to be here because if something happens, that's my job,' said one of them.

'Alright, what about you go back over by the door where you can still see us and if something happens you can be right there?' They agreed and stepped back, giving us some space.

'Kia ora,' I said to the whānau, 'my name is Timoti and I'm going to be helping extubate your boy and making sure he's safe when he comes around.' Their faces were like thunder, which was fair enough because the whole environment was tense.

I said to the mum: 'I couldn't help but notice your boy's name.' The brother moved as if to start advancing on me. 'I don't mean anything by it,' I said. I explained I didn't know the boy's namesake personally, and asked the whānau if they knew another person from the same chapter in Papakura. They did. I told them I'd grown up in south Auckland with that person and we'd been in prison together.

We started sharing stories about people we both knew, and everything mellowed out. Those personal connections, those shared experiences, just calmed the whole situation down.

Once the boy came around and everything was safe, I pulled his brother to one side. He would have been in his early twenties. I said: 'Hey bro, the reason I brought up those names and my connections is that I know where you are now. At the time I was your age, that was my life, and that's all I could see myself doing or becoming.'

I told him I'd never judge him for the life he was leading, whatever it was he was doing. 'Because I understand where you are,' I told him. 'But if you ever get to a point where you think maybe this life is not for you, now that you've met me you know you've got potential to do other things. And that's more than just working in a factory and struggling to put food on the table for your family. You have the ability to do a lot more, if you want to.' Even if that wasn't for him, I said, someday he'd probably have kids and I hoped he could see that they could have other futures beyond being in the cycle his whānau had been in for generations already.

'Sweet, bro,' he said to me. And he seemed to take it to heart. He listened. It was more than anyone else on the ward that day could have achieved.

I went and had something to eat; and when I came back, people on the ward had heard what had happened, how I'd defused the situation. The boss came up and shook my hand, and everyone was happy.

The thing was, I was comfortable talking with a gang whānau just as much as I was to consultants and the bosses. And I wanted to do that, to help in that way, to break down barriers. *This is where I want to be, this is what I want to be doing,* I thought to myself. It confirmed to me that I was doing the right thing; yes, sometimes it was hard, sometimes there was a lot of pressure, but it would all be worth it. I just had to keep going.

Besides, sometimes I felt like I had to be there as a counter to the prejudice and discrimination I witnessed. One day a guy from a gang came in with severe abdominal pain. It turned out to be acute appendicitis, so he was sent to surgery. I was in theatre with another student and the registrar surgeon, she was really cool. Then another registrar came in; he'd just been with the patient in the pre-op area, getting his consent to the operation. Immediately he started being a real wanker about the patient, being extremely arrogant, going on about him having a meth problem and making assumptions about him.

Next thing, the patient came in, in his gown, ready for surgery. He was a big boy, but he was extremely nervous. I tried to help calm him by talking with him. Noticing a tattoo on his arm, I mentioned a few of the guys I knew from his gang. We talked about people we both knew, connections we had; whakawhanaungatanga. It helped to set him at ease a bit.

But when it was time for the anaesthetic, he started freaking out about the medication, asking: 'What are you giving me?'

And the registrar replied: 'It's the same drug that killed Michael Jackson.'

What a fuckwit. I couldn't believe it. You have a duty of care to your patients; a duty to respect them no matter what you think of them.

\+ + +

The thing is, when you work in a hospital you never know who's going to come in the door and what their circumstances are.

One day when I was on the intensive care ward, a young Māori boy, also in a gang, was brought in after being hit on the head with a bat by some rivals. He wasn't in a good shape. There's a thing called a bolt which can get inserted into the head to read the pressure inside the brain, the intracranial pressure. It's important that this pressure is monitored and managed, because if it gets too high it means there's too much inflammation and the vessels of the brain get squeezed and squashed and blood can't get to where it needs to. If that happens, the brain can die.

This boy was on the ward being monitored via the bolt, and he'd been intubated to help him with his breathing. I walked past his cubicle and there was a young woman in there, who I assumed was his sister. She was crying and hugging him. Patients were only allowed two visitors at a time, and they had to be on a list and give their names when they arrived. Next thing, another young woman appeared; she was the patient's girlfriend. And I quickly discovered that the first young woman wasn't the guy's sister — she was his ex, and she'd snuck in using his current girlfriend's name.

It was all on. They were into each other, a full-on fight erupting right in the middle of intensive care. I jumped in between them and held them apart, telling the ex, 'You've gotta go.' She started laughing and headed for the door. I followed her to the door just to make sure there was no more trouble, which there wasn't. As I turned around at the end of the corridor, I could see the patient, out of it in a coma, not having a clue about the drama that had just unfolded and the two women fighting over him. I thought to myself: *This is probably the first time in history a Māori boy could say to his girl, 'Babe, I did nothing' — and be telling the truth!*

About three days later he had come back around and we were able to discharge him a few days after that. Before he went, I sat down with him and told him a bit of my story, and showed him the *I Am Innocent* documentary I was in. He'd done some time in prison, just like I had, and I explained that I knew a bit of what he was going through.

I told him, 'Bro, I know you'll be the same as me — you'll have this focus inside you, and a determination that no one is going to tell you any fucking thing. You can use that; you can use that. You just have to have the discipline to do it.' We hugged it out, and he left. I'll never know how things worked out for him. I hope he listened. Because the further I went on this road, the more I realised that the experiences I'd been through, the shit I'd endured, could be honed and turned and used in ways I could never have imagined.

I thought about something I'd learned at med school. We all have these molecules in our bodies called ROS, or reactive oxygen species. They're a byproduct of cellular respiration — cells use oxygen to make energy for themselves, and ROS is what's left over. They run around inside of us, and they can be really bad because they'll react with other things and cause trouble. If they become excessive, they can actually kill us.

But studies have shown that a mild increase in ROS actually helps the body become resilient. Therefore, despite the potential to be a bad influence they also have the ability to be positive, to make us stronger. And that's how I started thinking about the experiences I'd been through: yes, they could be super-toxic and destructive; but they could also be utilised to make me stronger and more resilient.

Instead of wallowing in regret, I'd come to know I would not be where I was without coming from there, without walking those steps; the same ones so, so many of my people have for decades. It made me more resolute, even more bent on continuing, even more single-minded about being the change.

Chapter 21

A Bad Smoothie and a Big Decision

Once we got to the end of the fifth year of med school, the second of my three years in Wellington, the exams were mostly behind us. The sixth year, or 'TI' (training intern) year, was where we got to do a lot more practical, hands-on doctoring. It felt like properly training to be a doctor. I did a bunch of cool stuff, like opening up someone's chest when I was on cardiothoracics.

One of the most memorable experiences came about during my final run in ICU, intensive care. We got a call about a woman in Palmerston North who had suffered something called a subarachnoid haemorrhage. In your skull there are three outer layers around the brain, and the subarachnoid is the middle layer.

A CT scan had showed up a mass of white, which indicated blood — a vessel had burst in there.

The plan was to fly her to Wellington for a neurosurgeon to open up the skull, clip the burst vessel to stop the bleeding, and for her to then be sent to us in ICU to be looked after from there. However, by the time she reached Wellington the plan had changed because the bleeding was so bad. Too bad to be going to the operating theatre, so she was sent straight to ICU. I accepted the patient on to the ward, explained to the boss what the situation was, and he said: 'Okay, we're going to have to have a difficult conversation with the whānau.' She wasn't going to survive.

We spoke to the whānau, explaining the situation and what would happen. The patient was in a coma and only being kept alive by the machines. The whānau made the decision to donate her organs, to give someone else a chance at extending their life; a most precious gift.

I asked the boss if I could be involved, watching what happened. It was an incredible experience. She was donating her heart, lungs, liver and both her kidneys, a process which took about a week, which gave the whānau time to say their goodbyes. During those five days, behind the scenes an army of coordinators arranged an array of logistics, as teams were assembled, recipients found and surgeries scheduled. Timing was everything.

Finally, I got a phone call to say it was happening — it was time for the retrieval, the operation to collect her organs. As usual for these operations, it happened in the middle of the night — often it's between midnight and 2 a.m., the quietest time for theatres. I went with her from the ward down to theatre where a team was waiting. Since her heart and lungs were going to be sent up to Auckland, a cardiothoracic team from there had flown to Wellington to collect the organs themselves.

While she was in a coma she was physically alive, so the first thing to happen was she needed anaesthetic. Once that happened, her torso was opened up and the surgical team began sectioning away the organs. Her heart was still pumping, the lungs inflating and deflating; these two incredible machines of nature doing their job, albeit with mechanical help.

Then the cardiothoracic surgeon reached for the aorta. Snip, snip, snip, he cut it away and then pulled it out. He handed it to a colleague who thoroughly checked its condition, making sure everything was okay, and placed it on ice. In the meantime, the surgeon had done the same with the lungs — snip, snip, snip, pull them out of the body they had served so relentlessly, so methodically, for decades.

Others had got to work on the other organs, carefully removing them while making sure they weren't trimming off the vessels too close. The surgeon with responsibility for the liver removed it, put it on ice, then beckoned to me to take a close look, talking me through what to look out for to make sure it was in good condition and viable for transplant.

Time flew by, and soon everything was done. I got to sew up the patient, whose body had done its job and was now going to help others whose organs were failing them. I then went home, grateful to have been part of a process that seemed miraculous.

There was one more stage I was going to get to be part of. After some sleep and a trip to the gym, I went back to work. Around six o'clock, I returned to theatre and observed as one of the kidneys I'd watched being removed from one patient only hours earlier was transplanted into another patient, another woman.

About five days later, I sat with her and had a cup of tea; this woman who had been given a new lease on life. It was beautiful. It was reminiscent of my circle-of-life day on the ambulances when I helped deliver a baby on one job and then ease another patient out of this world, comfortably and with dignity, on another.

This time the circumstances were different, but the sense was the same: being able to help and contribute to people's lives in this way made me feel good.

+ + +

There were other things that gave me the chance to contribute. During my studies I'd had a lot of help from the university's Māori support service, and they helped open up other opportunities too. At one point I talked with them about doing some research, and they connected me with a team doing an anaesthetic study looking at the effects of anaesthesia on patients post-surgery. It was led by a consultant and a senior registrar who were both great to work with.

We were looking at patients from day surgery and seeing how the drugs affected their sleep. Initially I had to help recruit participants for the study; we got 300, which was excellent.

But then I got tasked with something I initially thought was a bit stink, the dumb part of the study. I was involved in figuring out the best way to get responses from participants, and seeing if text messages were an effective tool. *What?!* It hardly seemed like cutting-edge science and research, but I got on with it — and in the end, it was very rewarding.

In terms of response rates, the text message method killed it. The results for Māori and Pasifika, who have notoriously low response rates, were exceptional. We got a response rate of 68% for that group; the next closest, via GP survey, was 12.5%. So, despite my initial misgivings it turned out to be a useful contribution, helping future researchers know how best to reach those communities. A future study trying to replicate it and understand *why* the participants responded could produce a gold standard for reaching indigenous communities around the world.

The study, 'The Day Surgery Sleep Survey (DURESS): Effect of day surgery on sleep quantity and quality', was published in the *British Journal of Anaesthesia*, with my name as one of the five researchers. Me — the kid who dropped out of school, lived on the streets, went to jail as a teenager — now a published researcher in a prestigious medical journal.

It was just another way I was proving that my past would not hold me back, that those who once sought to pull me down would never, ever succeed.

+ + +

During my final rotation in my sixth year, I got sent to a general medicine ward at Masterton Hospital. Masterton is a town in the Wairarapa region, over the other side of the Remutaka ranges from Wellington. It seemed a long, long way from south Auckland where I'd grown up, from any of the cities I'd lived in since, and I thought I'd hate it. A rural hospital in a rural town — what was there to like?

But I must admit it: Masterton, you got me. I really enjoyed it. The Māori service had a house right next to the hospital, with no rent, just a koha, so it was good, cheap living. All the bosses were really cool and I got to do some stuff I would never have expected.

One older woman came in with an infection in her gut caused by a bacteria called *Clostridium difficile*, or *C. diff*. It's an infection that usually hits people who've had too many antibiotics. The antibiotics' overuse kill the good gut bacteria, allowing the bad bacteria to grow unchecked. Because of that it's difficult to get control of, and in the meantime the patient suffers, putting up with diarrhoea and other distressing symptoms. The thing with *C. diff*, too, is that it can cause other complications because patients can end up dehydrated and with electrolyte imbalances due to the diarrhoea. Once that happens, it can cause kidney damage and also affect any other medications the patient might be on.

So it can be really dangerous.

The usual treatment is another antibiotic called vancomycin, a strong drug that is used for attacking superbugs and other resilient bacterial infections. So we put her on that, and kept her in hospital, hoping it would clear up. But it didn't work; she just wasn't coming right. Poor thing.

Then the boss, who was American, had another idea. 'We're going to do a faecal transplant,' he said. *A what now?* I thought. *Okaay.*

It works by taking faeces from a donor with a healthy gut and transferring it to the colon of the patient. That way, the good bacteria in the donor sample can fight back against the bad bacteria which have run rampant in the patient's gut due to the antibiotics.

We spoke to the patient and her family, and asked for a volunteer: who could donate some faeces? Her son put his hand up and we made the arrangements, after vetting him to make sure he — or at least his faeces — was a good candidate.

The day before the procedure, he dropped off his sample and we put it in the fridge — a special fridge, obviously, not the one in the staff cafeteria. Next morning we got out a blender — again, a special one, obviously — and put the donated sample in there with 300ml of saline solution and blended the shit out of it (pun intended). It was like a smoothie. I grabbed a rectal catheter from the supply room along with a syringe, and we were ready to go.

Our patient was placed in the foetal position throughout, and we had to do our best to be respectful since it was hardly the most dignified procedure. The boss placed the catheter and then handed me the syringe. I sucked up the 'smoothie' from the blender and began getting it to where it needed to be; I knew I had given enough when it began dribbling out. The patient had to stay in the foetal position for about another half hour to prevent the good bacteria from being evacuated (again, pun intended).

And once successfully anchored, the good bacteria began to colonise her gut.

A couple of days later, she was well enough to be discharged — it had worked.

Before I left that placement in Masterton, I got to do a presentation over Zoom to my classmates and an anaesthetist. The tutorial was on medication management and critical thinking with sick patients. It went well, and my tutor said it was the first time anyone from the school had done a presentation about a faecal transplant.

\+ + +

All the while I'd been studying and spending time in the hospital wards, doing rotations in the various specialities — from general medicine to paediatrics to mental health and everything in between — I'd been thinking about which one I might like to end up in some day. That choice was still some way off, but of course everyone spent time thinking about it.

As a newly qualified doctor you spend a minimum of two years as a house doctor, or junior doctor, before you can apply to start focusing on one area, one speciality. After many, many more years of working and training in that field, you can then apply to be a consultant. A career in medicine is a long and winding road, no doubt about it. When I'd first thought about being a doctor, emergency medicine seemed the obvious choice. After all, I'd had all that experience on the ambulances at the frontline of accidents and emergencies in the community, so it seemed natural to move into the hospital frontline. Then, even in my first couple of years at Otago, other specialities started to appeal. First, I really enjoyed surgery and I found I had the skills for it. So for a while there I thought I'd like to spend my time in operating theatres with a scalpel in hand.

But I came to realise that I shouldn't be guided just by what I enjoyed doing. This was something that I really started to think about after spending time with a paediatric surgeon. He was from the Cook Islands, we got on well, and he ended up giving me some of the best advice I'd ever received. First, he emphasised that you had to know the basics well; something he demonstrated to me during a surgery.

'Before you even start, you'd got to have a good understanding of the anatomy, you've got to know where things are,' he said. There was a boy of about eight years old who had a testicular torsion, who had come to the theatre to have it fixed. The surgeon said to me: 'Now, he's had imaging done and I've had a look at it, and I'm going to say the testicle is here.' And he made a mark on the patient. He opened up the patient and the testicle was right where he said it would be, right underneath the mark. His knowledge and skill and experience were obvious.

Afterwards, we were having lunch together and he asked me: 'Tim, what do you want to do when you become a doctor?'

'Something I enjoy, something that gives me a sense of purpose,' I replied.

'You should enjoy what you're doing, and it should give you a sense of wanting to get up and do it every day,' he said.

'But there's something else that's just as important, maybe even more important.'

He told me that whatever pathway I chose, I should have an express purpose of having an influence later on in my career. 'Otherwise, you'll build up knowledge, experience, understanding of your chosen field, but if you don't have any influence, you won't be in a position to change the things that need changing, to make things better,' he said. In that space, frustration grows, and you get fucked off. 'And then it becomes a cancer rather than a career,' he said.

It really struck a chord with me. I didn't go to medical school just to be a doctor: I wasn't after the certificate to hang on the wall, or the stethoscope to hang around my neck. *I wanted to make a difference.* The surgeon's words were a reminder that I needed to bear that in mind when I chose which field I went into; to make sure I went into it with the intention of having an influence when the time came.

Nobody wants to be a know-it-all from the get-go, of course. But, eventually, with knowledge and experience and skills built up over years, I wanted to be ready to make a difference, to *be* the difference, to be the change.

In a clinical sense, the area I was gravitating towards, the one that stood out, was intensive care. Dealing with patients who had high needs, whose lives were on the line; I began to feel that this was where I needed to be.

\+ + +

But choosing my preferred pathway, the field of speciality I'd end up in, was still a way away at this point. In the meantime, I needed to decide which area of the country I wanted to go to when I graduated. There wasn't much of a decision to be made here: I really wanted to go home, to where I'd grown up in south Auckland, to Middlemore Hospital, in the Counties Manukau health district.

Unfortunately, this is not as straightforward as going where you want. The process is like a dating app for doctors. At the end of the final year of med school you pick which districts you want to go to, listing at least six in order of preference. Then you put together your résumés to send to the districts, and hope for the best. Each of the districts you've nominated goes through your application, and they rank you — so you're ranking them, and they're ranking you. Swipe left, swipe right, left, right. At the end of it all, the system spits out matches, connecting candidates with districts. Then offers are sent out.

I was nervously waiting, and hoping, but it was all out of my control.

Another thing happening at the end of the final year was graduation. For me, it was cool — but a little bit anticlimactic.

First, since there were no big exams in our last year, once we'd finished the previous year it felt like we'd already made it. That sixth year as a TI was like a victory lap. Don't get me wrong: it was still hard work. But there wasn't the pressure of having exams to pass.

Also, unlike many of the other students, becoming a doctor wasn't the biggest goal of this journey I was on. Whereas most of the others were pumped and super-hyped — 'We did it!' — I was already thinking about what next. It felt good to achieve the goal and celebrate it with whānau and friends, but I already had my eyes looking forward. Graduating as Dr Timoti Te Moke was cool, but my real goal was to realise my potential, to follow the advice that paediatric surgeon had given me: to be in the position to influence a better world, for the country and for my people.

As the year ended, I found out where I was heading — *ding*, I got a match. And it was the one I wanted: Middlemore Hospital, in Counties Manukau.

Chapter 22

The Point of It All

Choosing to go home to south Auckland, to Middlemore Hospital, wasn't just about heading back to where I'd spent most of my childhood, like some sort of nostalgia trip. It was much more than that. I'd had it in my head for a long time that this was where I needed to be. Not for me, but for others — like that eight-year-old kid I saw on the pedestrian crossing in Papatoetoe.

Being a doctor in south Auckland, one who came from the background that I did, who had the experiences I did, could show others that there were different options than the ones they might be thinking about. I needed to normalise this, to do whatever I could to break down the barriers, to open people's eyes. That's why I chose to go to Middlemore after qualifying. But it was done with humility: I had no desire to be out there grandstanding. My intention was to walk the walk, to do my job, and through that be the change.

There was no need for me to be humbled. But when I came back to Auckland for the summer before starting work, I had to head to a Work and Income office to sign up for the dole. I had no work, no money and no home. In a way, it felt cathartic walking into the office, standing in line and waiting to see a case worker to explain my situation. Yeah, sure, I was due to start work as a doctor in the new year, but until then I was the same as everyone else, just trying to get by, relying on government assistance to be able to afford a place to rent and to buy food.

Soon enough, though, in the middle of January 2024, I had my first day at the hospital, one of about 60 new doctors going through induction and being welcomed with a mihi whakatau. I was excited, yet it was daunting, and I knew it was going to hurt sometimes. As the most 'experienced' junior doctor, aged 56, it was probably going to be harder for me than for my younger colleagues to cope with the inevitable long hours and night shifts. But I'd never been much of a sleeper anyway, getting by on about five hours a night, and I already had years of working night shifts when I was a paramedic, so I knew what I was in for.

Also, I'd had a lifetime of confronting tough situations. I was ready.

\+ + +

In the first few weeks there was so much to learn — Middlemore was like a city all by itself, with myriad systems to become familiar with, and a maze of corridors and wards and rooms to memorise so you didn't get lost.

And while in our final year of med school it sometimes felt like we'd already begun our careers as doctors, we always had someone with us. Now, I was on my own, albeit with supervision. If someone was sick and needed to see a doctor — that was me. If someone needed drugs to be charted — that was me. If someone needed an X-ray or a CT scan — that was me on the phone to radiology, hustling on behalf of my patient.

Once again I was able to directly care for people and have some autonomy, just as I'd wanted when I'd decided to become an ambulance paramedic. But after six years of studying medicine, I was now also equipped with the extra skills and knowledge I'd known I needed after that patient died and I came away feeling like I'd let her down.

As a junior doctor, a house surgeon, I was very much part of a team. When we did our rounds, and the consultant said the patient needed some procedure, drug or treatment, it was up to me to arrange that. Or if the registrar said, 'We need this', it was my job to make sure it got done. There was a hierarchy — consultant, registrar, house surgeon — and I was okay with that.

I was learning a bunch, including how things worked in a major hospital. Sometimes it seemed like a giant baton relay, spanning across shifts and departments, as we collaborated and figured out what was happening with a patient. Other times it was like being paid to solve puzzles, and my ability to think outside the square came to the fore.

There was one case where an Indian woman came into the hospital complaining of chest pain. One of the first things that happens in those cases is the patient will get a blood test. It's one way to detect if someone has had a heart attack. Her results were mostly clear, except they showed she was anaemic, meaning her haemoglobin levels were low. With everything else normal, she was sent home with the instruction to go back to her GP for another blood test soon.

About a week later, she went to the GP, who ordered a blood test and then rang her up and told her to go straight to hospital — her haemoglobin was now very low. Once she got to the emergency department they ran another test, and in just those few hours her haemoglobin levels had dropped *again*. What was going on?

I was on the final shift of my general medicine rotation, and was tasked with coming up with a plan to find out what was wrong and see if we could treat her. I discussed with the registrar supervising me the obvious possibilities, including heavy menstruation and certain cancers. I went to see the patient, examined her, asked her questions to screen for those conditions we suspected; but nothing was jumping out.

Then I asked: 'Are you taking any Ayurvedic medications?' Ayurveda is a form of traditional Indian medicine.

'Um, yes,' she and her husband replied. It turned out that when she first started having a sore chest, about six weeks earlier, she'd consulted an Ayurveda practitioner in India and he had sent her some medications.

I went back to my registrar: 'I think I've got it, mate.' We looked up the traditional medications she'd been taking and found that one of them contained lead. We ran some more blood tests — and discovered her lead levels were twenty times normal.

The registrar used the case in the weekly 'Grand Round', where senior doctors talk about unusual cases they've dealt with, and gave me credit for solving it.

It wasn't always that satisfying, of course. Sure, sometimes I made mistakes, things got dropped, or in the frenzy I'd forget something; as new doctors, we all did — hell, it happens to experienced practitioners, too. But the key is not to panic, not to freeze and let it overwhelm you. You take it on the chin, you learn from it, and you get on with your next job.

It was a super-stressful environment, for sure, sometimes to the point of being unhealthy. And yet I was often able to reflect: *This is nothing compared to what I've been through. There is nothing that could be thrown at me in this place which would even begin to compare with some of the stressful shit I've been through. It wouldn't even come close.*

I guess you could call that my superpower.

+ + +

At graduation from med school, when I'd held my excitement in check compared with others, it was because becoming a doctor was not the pinnacle achievement I'm striving for. Of course it's an important part, but I have so much else I want to achieve as well. And that includes the Waitangi Tribunal claim regarding racial bias in prosecutions.

I first lodged it back in 2016, and it's still making its way through the system. In 2022 there were hearings about how to proceed with it, and how to fund it, and I'm hoping there will soon be some real progress on the substance of the claim. Every day that goes by when there isn't an acknowledgement of bias and a genuine attempt to fix it — and keep it fixed — is another day when young Māori and Pasifika end up being targeted by police and dragged before the courts.

My own experience has shown that those early interactions with police, getting convicted for stupid shit, can have a cascading effect. Looking back at the 40 convictions I amassed between 14 and 21, I think: *Yes, I was a little shit.* But I wonder if another fourteen-year-old kid, one who wasn't Māori, would have been convicted for 'burgles other property under $100'?

It's easy to say that I was destined for trouble because of my bad home life. But that's far too simplistic — just as it is to say the police are the sole cause. Nothing happens in isolation. An abusive, poverty-stricken upbringing put me on the streets where I was vulnerable to the police. The police then piled conviction after conviction on me, knowing that each charge would increase the chances I'd end up in prison for a long, long time. No longer society's problem. I was never seen by the police as a vulnerable child or a victim of child abuse. They saw me as a criminal who needed to be charged and disciplined. Aged sixteen, I was sent to jail with gang members and inevitably ended up one myself.

Decades later, that attitude and the perception of me as a criminal continued, no matter what I did. When I was desperately trying to make a real difference to society and build a career as a paramedic, the police chose to charge me with manslaughter when I'd done nothing wrong.

The worst influence in my life has been the police.

I do not want that for future generations of Māori and Pasifika kids and I am determined to do what I can to stop it.

In the process of advancing the tribunal claim, my lawyer Roimata Smail and I have tried various tactics, including meeting directly with the police. That's how I ended up sitting down with the deputy police commissioner who would go on to become Commissioner of Police. I'd had this idea that rather than taking an adversarial approach, why didn't we get on the same page? We all wanted what's best for the betterment of Māori, right? My idea was that the police could become a co-claimant, be part of the case rather than us arguing. That way we could *really* make a difference.

The deputy police commissioner talked about all the things police were trying to do to correct the obvious imbalance in prosecution statistics; although in fact, it's not just prosecutions, it's across the board. From who gets stopped and searched, to use of force, to who gets offered diversion, to who gets sentenced to prison: it's all disproportionate against Māori and Pasifika.

Anyway he talked and I listened, and to be honest, it was the same spin I'd heard before. But I didn't say anything because I figured it was worth getting him on side. When the meeting was finished and he was about to leave, I said to him: 'There's a reason I'm here and it's different to what people might think. I could quite easily ride off into the sunset as a doctor with relative financial security. I could just become forever known as a poster child, "the little engine that could".'

I think he took it the wrong way, perhaps he thought I was implying the police would stop me, because he said: 'Well, you still can.'

I said: 'Of course I can, but that would do nothing for my people and do nothing for this country. I'm not here for me. If it was just about me, I wouldn't be here.' This was not about vengeance for what happened to me because of police decisions stretching back to when I was a teenager, let along being wrongly charged with manslaughter.

I think he got it.

After the meeting was over, and we'd promised to keep in touch, I got the idea of expanding this cooperative, co-claimant approach even further, and so my lawyers and I wrote to the Minister of Police and the Minister of Justice, inviting them to become part of the claim, too.

Justice wrote back saying it wasn't their role to do that, which was fair enough. But then I got a letter from the Crown lawyers and they were trying to dictate the way the claim was going to go, to hijack it. I don't like being pushed around — you might have guessed that by now. So that was the end of any attempt to have a claim with the Crown on board.

I did meet with the police commissioner another couple of times; he came to see me when I was in Dunedin as a med student. Once he tried to offer me some work within the police, but I wasn't interested in that at all. Our conversations were convivial, though. I put to him my suggestions for what needed to change, and he seemed to listen. For instance, I believed there needed to be an independent body that oversaw police decisions to prosecute Māori; a group of people whose job it was to audit bias and make non-binding recommendations.

I got the feeling that if it was up to him, he'd consider implementing the ideas. But to do so required compromises he wasn't prepared to make. In a way, I could see that he was like me when I held an influential position in the bikie club in Australia. At all times I needed to be aware of people's perceptions of me, and I also needed to be looking out for those who wanted my job. Everything I wanted to do had to be run through those lenses first: how would my actions have an impact on the perceptions of others, both those who followed me and those who were ready to stab me in the back at the first opportunity? I sensed that as much as he might have wanted to make generational change in terms of police treatment of Māori, he was stymied by how it would be perceived within the ranks, and how it would be weaponised against him by his enemies.

The thought of a seventeen-year-old me looking on as adult me sat down with a Commissioner of Police requires a bit of mind-bending. At that age, there was no way I would have been anywhere near such a meeting — I was fully indoctrinated into the world I was living in then, one of violence, abuse, gangs and prison. I had been through so much and been dragged back and forth to court by the police, even had a police dog used against me as a weapon. There were times when I wanted to be killed by police in a big shoot-out.

So, no. That situation would never have happened.

In many ways, I still have the same prejudices against the police that I did back then. I still distrust them and I'm still pissed off at the way brown people of this country are treated in our justice system. But I have evolved. Perhaps ironically, some of the skills I learned in the bikie club in Australia — of brinkmanship and negotiation — have taught me that it's better to sit down with people and talk with them, to discuss the issues that divide you. To be able to speak, even to your enemies, and say: 'Here's where we need to get to.' To have a conversation.

I'm now on a crusade to benefit Māori — all Māori — which will benefit the whole country. And the police are an integral part of that. So if we could be on the same side, and do business together to achieve that benefit, why wouldn't I want that?

Maturity and life experience can teach you a lot.

+ + +

Remember how there's that place I can stand at my tūrangawaewae, at the urupā next to my marae, where I can look over the fence and know that buried within Papatūānuku are tūpuna going back hundreds of years? And that when I stand there, I understand that I am a link in a very, very long chain?

I have that understanding now because I know my whakapapa. It's a comfort. And it's a responsibility. Because for me the question is: what does all this mean for the future, for those links in the chain beyond me?

The answer is that as a link in the chain, I want to create and sustain change now and into the future, to help people well beyond my lifetime. I have overcome so much to get to this point, and now I have an obligation to create change for good; to overturn stereotypes and assumptions; to flip discrimination and racism on its head; to show that everyone deserves the opportunity to fulfil their true potential.

I don't hold any bitterness about what I have endured. I am the quintessential product of all the negative social determinants, and I've overcome them. And doing that has made me who I am today — an unstoppable force on a path to create a bright future for Māori and therefore the whole country. Like that paediatric surgeon said, I shouldn't go into something without having the intention to have influence in years to come. That's the plan; that's why I keep going and keep striving. If I just stopped and said, 'Okay, great, I've made it', I'd be short-changing myself, not realising my true potential, not helping others.

So I will keep going, creating change in such a way that when it's time for me to leave the earth, the world will know my name; the world will be a better place because I was here.

Acknowledgements

I would like to start by acknowledging two of my tūpuna and namesakes: Te Moke from my koro's side and Aperehama from my nana's side.

My next acknowledgements are of course to my koro, Nīkora Karora, and my nana, Mākareti Dunsdale. They are the reason I am who I am today.

To my brother Matthew, I apologise for not knowing how to be the brother I was meant to be.

To the rest of my whānau, particularly my cousins, thank you all.

Mary Kayes and the entire Kayes family — Paul, Beth, Anne, Ruth, James and Rachel — thank you.

To Otago University, and in particular Otago Medical School, for your courage to empower Māori and for all the support you gave me.

To Roimata Smail, Erin James and Tim McKinnel, for being an integral part of my journey for the betterment of Māori and this country.

To Eugene Bingham, Michelle Hurley, Kate Grimstock and the team at Allen & Unwin Aotearoa New Zealand, for helping me write and publish this book.

And finally, to my son, Kaha Te Moke. Thank you for giving me what I had been seeking from my father my entire life.